TOWARD A NEW COMMON SCHOOL MOVEMENT

Critical Interventions
Politics, Culture, and the Promise of Democracy

A Series from Paradigm Publishers

Edited by Henry A. Giroux, Susan Searls
Giroux, and Kenneth J. Saltman

TOWARD A NEW COMMON SCHOOL MOVEMENT

NOAH DE LISSOVOY
ALEXANDER J. MEANS
KENNETH J. SALTMAN

Paradigm Publishers
Boulder • London

KH

Copyright © 2014 Paradigm Publishers

Published in the United States by Paradigm Publishers,
5589 Arapahoe Avenue, Boulder, CO 80303 USA.

Paradigm Publishers is the trade name of Birkenkamp & Company,
LLC, Dean Birkenkamp, President and Publisher.

Library of Congress Cataloging-in-Publication Data

De Lissovoy, Noah, 1968-
 Toward a new common school movement / Noah De Lissovoy,
Alexander J. Means, and Kenneth J. Saltman.
    pages cm
 Includes index.
 ISBN 978-1-61205-440-7 (hardcover : alk. paper)
 ISBN 978-1-61205-432-2 (Institutional eBook)
 1. Public schools. I. Means, Alexander J., 1977– II. Saltman,
Kenneth J., 1969– III. Title.
 LA212.D45 2013
 371.010973—dc23

                                            2013022327

Printed and bound in the United States of America on acid-free
paper that meets the standards of the American National Standard
for Permanence of Paper for Printed Library Materials.

18 17 16 15 14 1 2 3 4 5

9/8/15

Contents

◇

Preface

From the natural world to the social world, the commons appear everywhere in peril. The all-encompassing drive for profit and endless commodification is despoiling the shared basis of life on the planet, and as a set of global crises widen and deepen, demands for authentic democracy and community become the minimal demands for the survival of society. Global economic desperation, ecological devastation, and political repression all require an urgent, intelligent, and original response. Any adequate effort to overcome these challenges will have to start from the premise of our belongingness, globally, to each other—the myriad ways we are in relation, and are produced out of these relations, and the myriad ways in which, in the context of continuing globalization, we will come to be even more so. This fundamental social condition of interrelation, collaboration, and entanglement sets the parameters for any meaningful global community. What we refer to as *a new common school movement* is the form of education that sets its sights on the development and democratization of this condition.

In recent years, scholars in the social sciences and humanities, along with activists and social movements, have sought to rejuvenate a discourse of the global commons as both a critique of the neoliberal expropriation of public and natural resources and a rallying cry for a different politics suitable to the unique challenges of the contemporary moment. Michael Hardt and Antonio Negri suggest that the global commons, or what they refer to simply as the common, is constituted by the totality of the public goods and natural resources that we all share as well as the realm of culture and immaterial production.[1] Public schools are firmly grounded in both sides of this equation, representing a vital public good that is deeply implicated in the production of knowledge, ideas, values, ways of being, and social relations crucial to democratic life. While the original common school movement associated with Horace Mann remains an important referent in the history of progressive education, researchers and theorists in educational studies haven't thought much about the common lately. *Toward a New Common School Movement* reads contemporary perspectives on the global commons as a frame for rethinking contemporary educational theory, politics, and practice. This requires recovering progressive elements of the original common school movement while reimagining them in relation to current educational conflicts and struggles.

Today, the very idea of public schooling is everywhere under assault from forces of privatization and enclosure. This takes the form of for-profit educational management, chartering, vouchers, standardization of curriculum, incessant high-stakes testing, and the integration of corporate managerialism into the fabric of teacher education, educational leadership, and schools themselves. Imagining public schooling as a commons is one way of avoiding what we refer to as the "blackmail" of neoliberalism, which frames as our only options a business agenda of deregulated market sovereignty, unresponsive state domination of the public, or an uncritical liberal accommodation to the existing economic and political order. We suggest that engagement with an *educational commons* opens a different space for reimagining the public and public schooling outside of the false choice between market imperatives and state domination, and instead locates questions of educational value and organization within the principles of human equality and global commonality. *Toward a New Common School Movement* is an effort to strengthen and reconceptualize public schooling for a genuinely democratic society beyond the crisis and failure of neoliberalism. We don't merely need to defend public schooling; we need to remake it. We believe that engagement with the theory and practice of the global commons provides a set of creative and ethical referents suitable to this task.

Reclaiming schooling for the commons is at once an economic and a political project, as well as a cultural, pedagogical, and curricular one. We consider all of these aspects in what follows, and in the process challenge the tendency in scholarship on education to fragment schools, teaching, and learning into isolated processes. We also place the proposal that we develop here in historical and social context. We consider both the history of thought on the idea of common schooling and the internal and external obstacles that it has confronted, and we describe the essential characteristics of the contemporary neoliberal turn, which powerfully reproduces and intensifies processes of class and racial domination in education, and against which our argument is directed. Finally, we describe several important principles and initiatives that could serve to unite and ignite a new common school movement.

We aim here to contribute to what is already a larger conversation. Although neoliberalism remains dominant, globally people are fighting back. In education in particular, there has recently been an encouraging upsurge of protest in the United States and internationally against contemporary regimes of privatization and austerity; these protests have engaged broadening circles of students, teachers, and communities. We hope that the present intervention can contribute to this emergent movement, and help it to find its way forward against the difficult forces that confront it.

◇

CHAPTER 1

Beyond the Failure
of Neoliberal Schooling

Over the past three decades in the United States, a corporate consensus has emerged in the media and among the elite that has declared public schooling to be a failed experiment—an antiquated institution incapable of meeting the demands and assorted crises of the global era. The problem is said to be located in the inefficient and corrupt nature of the public sphere itself and supposedly greedy and incompetent teachers and their unions. Across a network of high-profile corporate reform advocates, right-wing think tanks, business groups, and corporate foundations, it is suggested that the future of the nation depends on dismantling public school systems by subjecting them to commercial management and the discipline of market forces. The stated aim is to break up the "public school monopoly" through the wholesale privatization of the educational commons. This movement represents a form of enclosure that has sought to reframe the structure and value of public education within a narrow horizon of human capital development and the private concern of business to accumulate profit.

In this chapter, we consider the relationship between educational privatization and three conceptualizations of education for social justice. The first is the neoliberal (or market fundamentalist) conception of education for social justice that is dominant and expanding today (although proponents of neoliberal education have hijacked the

1

language of social justice, in reality, it is antithetical to social justice in part because it empties out the very notion of the social from public discourse).[1] The second is a liberal conception of education for social justice that was dominant prior to the ascendancy of neoliberal ideology and that is put forward by liberals and many progressives as preferable to corporate school reform.[2] The third is a theoretical/critical pedagogical conception of education for social justice. This discussion is undertaken to demonstrate the need for a reengagement with the global commons in educational theory and reform.

Neoliberal Privatization and Social Justice

Globally, in the past thirty years, understanding public school transformation apart from the dominant ideological trend of neoliberalism has become impossible. Neoliberalism, a form of radical fiscal conservatism, alternately described as "neoclassical economics" and "market fundamentalism," originates with Friedrich Von Hayek, Milton Friedman, and the "Chicago boys" at the University of Chicago in the 1950s. Within this view, individual and social ideals can best be achieved through the "unfettered market." In its ideal form, neoliberalism calls for privatization of public goods and services, deregulation of trade and finance, and the loosening of labor and environmental protections by the state. In the view of neoliberalism, public control over public resources should be shifted out of the hands of the necessarily bureaucratic state and into the hands of the necessarily efficient private sector.

In industrialized nations, educational privatization takes the form of for-profit management of schools, "performance contracting," for-profit and nonprofit charter schools, school vouchers, school commercialism, for-profit online education, online homeschooling, test publishing and textbook industries, electronic and computer-based software curricula, for-profit remediation, and educational contracting, to give but a partial list. The modeling of public schooling on business runs from classroom pedagogy that replicates corporate culture to the contracting out of management of districts, the corporatization of curricula, and the "partnerships" that schools form with the business "community" that aim to market to kids.

In developing nations, (low-fee) for-profit schooling is increasingly promoted by institutions like the World Bank, International Monetary Fund, World Trade Organization, and academics such as James Tooley (darling of the World Bank). In Tooley's book *A Beautiful Tree*, published by the free-market think tank CATO, he relies heavily on anecdotal bashing of public schooling, anecdotal celebration of private schooling, and a number of other unsubstantiated and contradictory assumptions. Tooley claims that private schools are superior in quality and more ethically driven than public schools. He argues that this is because of the market incentives for educational entrepreneurs to start schools and also the desire of educational entrepreneurs to gain social status and to do social work as philanthropists. However, Tooley concludes *A Beautiful Tree* by calling for foreign capital to build franchises of standardized for-profit schools in developing countries to compete against domestic low-fee private schools (McDonald's is the model). He argues that public money should be put into branding and advertising because of the supposed virtues of standardized schools and their brands, and that private philanthropic money should go not to support public schooling but to support forms of schooling for which profit can be drained out for investors. The basis for Tooley's romantic picture of privatization is the existing local low-fee private school, which he first uses to justify radical expansion of privatization. He then calls for foreign direct investment so that the schools in poor nations can be transformed on the model of the fast food industry. Tooley fails to deal with the fact that educational development modeled on the fast food industry would utterly transform both the local low-fee schools and the suggested status-based incentives for running private schools that he celebrates and that justify his argument. Tooley calls for ending public education, not for strengthening it or developing it where it is absent. The postscript reveals that Tooley has accepted a job as a manager of a $100 million education investment fund that stands to profit from the proliferation of for-profit schooling in the developing world.[3]

Tooley's view coincides with those of the three Bs: rock star Bono, Bill Gates, and Bill Clinton, who preach a new

"Gospel of Wealth," in which the only way to do good is for the super-rich to do well. Educational access can only be achieved in their view by creating the conditions for investor profit. Their views differ, however, from the original liberal Gospel of Wealth promoted by Andrew Carnegie, who called on the rich to give to support public knowledge-making institutions like libraries, museums, and schools so that the individual could have the opportunity for self-improvement through free access to information. The three Bs promote the privatization of access and production of knowledge and information: Gates, having made the largest fortune on the planet through commercializing the freely exchanged software in the hippy tech movement of the 1970s, pushes educational privatization through venture philanthropy; Bono tries to fight free exchange of music and cultural production as he and his bandmates squirrel away their millions in tax avoidance schemes in the Netherlands; and Bill Clinton pushes the post-political denial of ideology and politics that characterized his presidency and the private sector approach to philanthropy that dominates his Clinton Global Initiative. Although neoliberalism putatively denies politics, as David Harvey emphasizes, it should actually be understood as a tool of class warfare waged by the rich on the rest. The prominence and post-political orientation of the three Bs suggest that analysis of educational privatization has to comprehend the role of mass media, publicity, and public relations in shaping educational reform debates globally.

Neoliberalism appears in the now commonsense framing of education exclusively through the language and logic of the market—that is, private economic gain (the promise of cashing in knowledge for jobs) and global economic competition. Margaret Thatcher's TINA thesis (There Is No Alternative to free-market governance) has infected educational thought. The only questions on neoliberal educational reform agendas appear to be how to enforce knowledge and curriculum conducive to national economic interests and the expansion of a corporately managed model of globalization as conceived from the perspective of business and the political elite. Education, in this view, is seen as little more than a means of accommodating the student to the existing social order. Excluded from this perspective are the role of democratic participation in societies ideally committed to democracy and the role of public schools in preparing public democratic citizens with the tools for meaningful and participatory self-governance. Also excluded is the pursuit of global justice in forms that break with neoliberal globalization, such as the global justice movement and other grassroots movements for justice. By reducing the politics and ethics of education largely to economics, neoliberal educational reform has deeply authoritarian tendencies that are incompatible with democratic social relations, popular power, and the intellectual tools for social criticism as the basis for just social change. The authoritarian tendencies of neoliberal educational reform stem in part from the modeling of the school and school reform on the corporation, a decidedly hierarchical institution organized by authoritarian rather than egalitarian relations. These tendencies stem as well from the neoliberal ethical egoist vision of the individual as motivated by selfishness or self-interest and a vision of the social understood through the paradigm of social Darwinian competition. There is little room in this view for an understanding of the ways that individual ethical choices are informed by institutional contexts, nor is there much sense of the historical struggles for justice that have been waged by workers, women, and other historically marginalized individuals and groups to create better living and working conditions. These struggles have been waged not out of the ethos of competitive individualism characteristic of neoliberalism but rather out of ethical convictions, often-radical critiques of existing institutions and practices, and demands for justice and broad-based equality and solidarity.

Globally, a declaration of public system failure undergirds the claims for radical market-based restructuring and the transformation of public institutions and services as private deliverables. These representations are important for how they shift educational provision to the private field of business competition, excluding the public dimensions of schooling, including civic and ethical dimensions. In light of the devastation wrought by the financial crisis of 2008, the neoliberal tenets of unfettered deregulation and privatization have become universally discredited. The vast outward expansion of free-market governance over the last thirty years has not produced broadly shared prosperity or even social efficiency, but rather a radical expansion of social inequality, human insecurity, and institutional dysfunction. Nonetheless, unfazed, the neoliberal perspective continues to reimagine public education as a private market that will necessarily benefit from competition, choice, privatization, and commercialism even as the evidence continues to mount that these prescriptions are producing the very symptoms of failure they claim to mitigate. Knowledge and schooling are increasingly framed as responsible for saving capitalism. At the same time, the neoliberal vision for education fosters an abdication of the social altogether as education is positioned as the means for individuals to negotiate what Zygmunt Bauman calls "the individualized society."[4]

The Liberal Conception of Education for Social Justice

The liberal philosophical tradition from John Locke to John Rawls emphasizes the role of education in making the autonomous individual and preparing the citizen for political participation in the existing political system proper. Education appears as a means of individual humanistic edification and the basis for individual upward economic mobility. Within the liberal tradition, education facilitates the accommodation of the individual in the existing economic and political order. The liberal tradition tends to approach schooling, knowledge, and curriculum as the pursuit of universal truth and the accumulation of neutral knowledge. Power struggles over claims to truth and their relationship to the claimants are not a part of the liberal view. Consequently, education is perceived as a largely apolitical endeavor. The crucial issue becomes the effective transmission of an accumulated body of knowledge through "good schooling," which can be measured through "student achievement." While liberal approaches to schooling vary in their embrace of the equation of student achievement with testing, the claim to universal value and neutrality of knowledge results in a conception of knowledge as static and transmissible. Hence, the perspective on educational privatization tends to focus on efficacy of delivery. Privatization initiatives are most often viewed as a potential tool or threat to increasing effective delivery.

Linda Darling-Hammond, perhaps the most influential liberal educational policy scholar, typifies this position by calling for a depoliticized view of the content of schooling by declaring the need for an end to the "destructive curriculum wars" (that is, rejecting a political understanding of how it is that what schools do relates to broader social forces) and arguing instead for a focus on access to "expert teachers," "high-quality curriculum opportunities," "good educational materials," and so on.[5] On the one hand, for Darling-Hammond and other liberals, the curriculum and pedagogical approaches should be viewed as outside of politics, yet when it comes to defining what is meant by "expert," "good," or "high-quality," political values are of course smuggled back in. In Darling-Hammond's case, the project for liberal educational inclusion and access collapses into a vision of national economy and global economic competition that seeks to make sure that the American Empire doesn't fall the way Rome fell.[6]

The liberal tradition tends to affirm structures of power as unquestionable (capitalism paired with the liberal state) and seeks to utilize education as a means to greater assimilation. Social justice in this view is dominated by the logic of educational inclusion and the ideal of ameliorating or tweaking existing systems to make them more inclusive. If only more citizens can be educated, then they can be included in the economy, the political system, and the dominant culture. However, unlike neoliberalism, the liberal tradition tends to value the public sector as part of a just democracy. Educational privatization, contracting, and market-based experiments largely appear within these assumptions as potential tools to further public ends. Liberals tend to be skeptical of aspects of privatization, such as school commercialism, for tainting the otherwise allegedly neutral space of learning. They tend to be skeptical of privatization initiatives that drain public resources from the public system. They are also leery of neoliberal privatization efforts to remove teachers' unions and crush local governance in the form of school boards. However, the issue of efficacy of delivery trumps all.

The liberal view tends to assume that equality is defined by equality of opportunity. What they mean by "equal opportunity" is ultimately the responsibility of the individual to use freely available knowledge to better the self by competing on a largely level playing field. If the playing field is not exactly level, then it can always be leveled through a little tinkering. However, as Stanley Aronowitz writes, equality of opportunity presumes class inequality as a social norm. Aronowitz and other advocates of critical approaches to education contend that inequality should not be presumed as a social baseline and that education should be about creating the conditions for radically democratic social relations with regard to politics, culture, and economics.[7] Aronowitz's point is that the rhetoric of "access to opportunity" has resulted in naturalizing a durably unequal social order. Educational "access to opportunity" has become a fixture in political rhetoric at the same time that class mobility has significantly declined over the last several decades. Is it the responsibility of teachers, schools, administrators, and parents to magically counter the upward redistribution of wealth by teaching better? Are more efficient teaching methods going to provide an antidote to class exploitation or to rapidly expanding inequalities in wealth and income or to massive child poverty rates? In this regard, while often claiming the mantle of the historic progressive tradition in education, contemporary educational liberalism generally departs from it in refusing to argue for a broader and deeper process of social reconstruction in which democratic education would participate. In addition, although many liberals do contemplate the use of public measures to ameliorate numerous social ills, they tend to lack an understanding of how cultural symbolic hierarchies are intertwined with material inequalities.[8]

Liberal and conservative perspectives on public schooling operate through accommodationism. That is, they presume that we live in a fundamentally fair, open, and just social order and that the role of public schools is to accommodate students to that order. Although historically and presently state-administered public schooling is a site of contestation, both privatization and the ideology of corporate culture deepen the conservative tendencies of public schooling rather than unsettling them. Cultural conservatism (typified by E. D. Hirsch and the common core curriculum trend) with its dogmatic view of knowledge has a natural affinity with neoliberal ideology, because canonized claims to truth can be more easily standardized, tested, and mass marketed. The business model appears in schools in the push for standardization and routinization with emphases on standardization of curriculum, standardized testing, methods-based instruction, teacher de-skilling, scripted lessons, and a number of approaches aiming for "efficient delivery" of instruction. The business model presumes that teaching, like factory production, can be forever speeded up and made more efficient through technical modifications to instruction and incentives for teachers and students, like cash bonuses. While today's liberals object to the excesses of this regime, they generally do not dispute the positivistic understanding of learning and the preoccupation with "effectiveness" that underlie it. Holistic, critical, and socially oriented approaches to learning that understand pedagogical questions in relation to power are eschewed as privatization and corporatization instrumentalize knowledge, disconnecting it from the broader political, ethical, and cultural struggles informing interpretations and claims to truth while denying the ability of differential forms of material power to make meanings.

The Critical Perspective and the Need for the Commons

For critical theorists, the defense of public schools against neoliberal privatization is typically presented as a defense of the public sector with the goal of enhancing human freedom and democracy. The critical position emphasizes that public schools are sites of cultural struggle within civil society as well as sites for the making of critical consciousness. These distinctions concerning cultural struggle and critical consciousness are crucial and distinct from the liberal perspective. From a critical perspective, schools can be democratic public spheres that can foster public values, critical dispositions, and habits of an engaged citizenry. The critical perspective emphasizes that schools have the potential to make radical democratic subjects capable of engaging in such projects as democratizing the economy, strengthening the public roles of the state, challenging oppressive institutions and practices, and participating in democratic culture. Moreover, from a critical perspective, knowledge is subject to interrogation with regard to relations of power, and to questions of politics, history, and ethics. Critical theorists insist that experience needs to be questioned in relation to broader social, cultural, and political conditions, forces, and realities. From the critical perspective, ideally such critical examination of subjective experience in relation to objective forces becomes the basis for agency and action directed at democratic transformation of oppressive forces and structures.

From both a liberal and a critical perspective, the privatization of public schools and the ideology of corporate culture need to be opposed. However, one of the consequences of the neoliberal turn in education has been to put both liberals and critical educators on the defensive. In broader educational debates, the forces of conservative reaction have become the "progressives" by promoting "choice" and market "competition" in public educational systems. Conversely, those traditionally critical of the status quo in public schooling have become the conservatives, left to defend a public educational system everywhere under assault from the forces of privatization and profiteering. Missing here is an acknowledgment of how the subordination of educational systems to market rationalities and corporate dominance reflects broader struggles over the future of the commons and thus the very possibility of sustainable and democratic control over public and natural wealth for collective benefit. Neoliberal schooling represents not merely better or worse school reform—adjusting pedagogical methods, tweaking the curriculum, and so on. We argue that it is crucially about redistributing control over social life and as such is part of a much broader trend—the enclosure of the global commons.

Although the perspective we develop here belongs to the critical tradition, we also aim to extend this tradition through engagement with the global commons as a site of both conceptual dynamism and social and political possibility. Our vision for a new common school movement is rooted in the democratic potential embodied within our shared relationship to the commons—the thick mesh of resources, capacities, aspirations, and values that make up and divide our world. The antagonism at the heart of the global commons today is between the fundamental truth of human dignity and equality, on the one hand, and the proliferation of new walls, hierarchies, and forms of enclosure, on the other. On one side of this antinomy is the very foundation and possibility of democratic politics and thus a future in common, and on the other side, its calculated denial. The political is therefore always a struggle over competing visions of our global commonality—our responsibility to one another and our relationship to the commons. It is this struggle, we believe, that is under way in schools in the present. The question is whether we will continue to suffer the distorted and truncated forms of community that mainstream educational policy and practice impose on us or whether we will fight against the limits of the neoliberal imagination to realize authentically democratic forms of teaching and learning. In the following chapter, we describe contemporary challenges to education emerging from within processes of global enclosure and resistance.

◇

CHAPTER 2

From the Commons
to the Common

The moment of globality, and the sense of the common in this context, have to be thought of politically as well as ethically; we have to consider the meanings of both global democracy and community and their implications for education. This historic moment is inspiring to the extent that it represents an exhilarating new horizon for experiments in democracy and human relationships; it is menacing to the extent that it represents a powerful extension of sovereignty. There is nothing inherently liberating about the globalization of the economy, culture, and politics, since new instruments of control are evolving to accommodate and exploit this underlying historical transformation through the formation of supranational groupings of political and economic elites. On the other hand, if the democratic potential of this new horizon can be appropriated, its possibilities are equally unprecedented. We increasingly, if unevenly, inhabit a common globality. All depends on how, and to what end, that condition is inflected.

A crucial starting point for an analysis of the challenges to education posed by globalization, and for the proposal of a pedagogical project adequate to this moment, is the notion of *the common as collectively shared production, experience, and activity*. To grasp this sense of the common, the Marxian analytical tradition, and critical studies of globalization in particular, is especially helpful. Not only does this

12

framework make it possible to understand the formation of the common in political and economic terms, but also, in its contemporary articulations, it allows us to imagine fundamentally new senses of what the common might come to mean in the global era.

An initial point of reference for the common is the *commons* itself. For much of human history, land, water, and other natural resources were organized as a commons so that the elements necessary to sustain life were held and valued as collective property. Historically, the commons cannot be separated from the notion of *enclosure*, which signals efforts to transfer aspects of the commons from collective management to private ownership. In perhaps the most famous defense of enclosure and privatization of the commons, Garrett Hardin argued in "The Tragedy of the Commons" that without private property the commons inevitably become exploited and exhausted.[1] He used the metaphor of cattle, suggesting that individual owners will allow their own cattle to deplete the commons to maximize their individual gain. However, as David Harvey has observed, rather than a powerful argument for enclosure, what "The Tragedy of the Commons" ultimately demonstrated is that it was private ownership in cattle and the drive to maximize private utility that eroded the commons—if the cattle were held in common, the problem would cease to exist.[2] As Nobel economist Elinor Ostrum has detailed, rather than creating states of regulatory dysfunction, communities have historically developed ingenious strategies and rules governing access and usage of common property resources to maintain their collective value and benefit over time.[3]

The contemporary discourse of enclosure is derived largely out of Marxist historiographical perspectives that have traced the role of the original land enclosure movements during the transition from feudalism to capitalism in the sixteenth century. At the end of the first volume of *Capital*, Marx extended the perspectives of Adam Smith, who famously described the enclosure of the commons in feudal Europe as a form of *original* or *primitive accumulation*.[4] Whereas Smith argued that this was largely a peaceful historical passage, Marx detailed how the enclosures constituted a form of theft and violence that made the original development of capitalism possible. Marx observed a wide range of processes associated with primitive accumulation, including the commodification and privatization of land; the conversion of common, collective, and state property rights into private property rights; the forceful imposition of wage labor on commoners through their separation from the commons; and European colonialism and imperialist expansion. As historians like Peter Linebaugh have shown, the forces of primitive accumulation and the enclosures of the commons in feudal Europe gave birth to the proliferation of modern economic, legal, cultural, administrative, and military systems of sovereignty that legitimated private domination over the natural commons and European colonial domination over the world's lands, cultures, and peoples.[5] Silvia Federici's work has also alerted us to how women and women's reproductive labor have always been central to this story. From the European witch hunts to the current neoconservative war on women, women's bodies, their reproductive health, and their paid and unpaid labor have been a longstanding historical target of enclosure and control.[6]

Marx's preliminary thoughts on primitive accumulation situated it largely as an accomplished historical process unique to the transition from feudalism to capitalism. This has proven to be a limitation. As a system defined by perpetual growth and the endless pursuit of surplus value, capitalism is periodically prone to crisis and stagnation. Therefore, it must continually incorporate new territories, markets, and laborers into its orbit in order to survive. In relation to the commons, this underscores the point that capitalism must periodically convert shared social resources that have previously existed outside its domain into sources of private property and profit. Massimo De Angelis, David Harvey, and others have observed that this process of enclosure has reemerged on a planetary scale since the onset of neoliberal globalization in the 1980s and 1990s. As Slavoj Žižek points out, there are three crucial enclosures of the commons at present:

> *the commons of culture*, the immediately socialized forms of "cognitive capital," primarily language, our means of communication and education, but also the shared infrastructure of public transport, electricity, the postal system, and so on;
> *the commons of external nature*, threatened by pollution and exploitation (from oil to rain forests and the natural habitat itself);

the commons of internal nature (the biogenetic inheritance
of humanity); with new biogenetic technology, the creation of
a New Man [sic] in the literal sense of changing human nature
becomes a realistic prospect.[7]

A fourth enclosure of the commons involves the de facto
apartheid situation of new "walls and slums" that physically
enclose people, separating the excluded from the included
in the vast territories of poverty and human immiseration
that define the global present. These four enclosures of
the commons are being struggled over, and the stakes in
the struggle are, for Žižek, the very survival of the species
and the planet itself. Capitalist enclosure of the natural
commons produces ecological catastrophe. Global climate
change is only the most dramatic instance of the systemic
destruction caused by capitalism's inability to confront
natural limits. Capitalist enclosure of the knowledge commons makes ideas into private property rather than freely
shared and exchanged knowledge for potential universal
benefit. Thus, even public universities have undertaken, as
a central function, the commercialization of the research
and ideas produced through the collaborative work of
students and faculty. Capitalist enclosure transforms the
biological information that is the stuff of life into property—as can be seen in attempts by corporations to patent
genomes or organisms—setting the stage for new forms of
bio-slavery and profit-based control. These enclosures are
being extended into the context of public schooling as well.
For example, following Hurricane Katrina, neoliberal econo-
mists and education policy think tank fellows, political
consultants, and businesspeople used the storm to justify
privatizations and dismantling of public schools and public housing; dispossession of poor African Americans from
large sections of the city; imposition of voucher, contracting, and chartering schemes throughout the region; and
the firing and de-unionizing of the teacher workforce. In
education, Saltman has termed this primitive accumulation
and enclosure "capitalizing on disaster."

Also central to the educational sphere under neoliberalism is a process of enclosure of the *imagination*. Theorists
have proposed the notion of *cognitive capitalism* to indicate a
new and privileged source of surplus value in contemporary

capitalism: knowledge, affect, and intellect.[8] The knowledge industries, as well as the education sector, have become a crucial battleground in the struggle between the commodifying imperative of neoliberalism and the emancipatory impulses of individuals and communities. This struggle can be seen on the one hand in present efforts to remake education as both immediate source of profit (e.g., through the commodification of curriculum in schools or research in higher education) and reorganization of subjectivity and learning in terms of the production of human capital, and on the other hand in the efforts of students and educators to challenge this process. As capitalism colonizes the social field, including the affective and intellectual capacities of subjects, resistance comes to include a defense of the imagination, collective intelligence, and capacity for relationships of human beings. In this context, if an alternative to capitalism often seems unthinkable in the present, this is because thinking itself has become increasingly captured by and embedded in circuits of capitalist production and valorization.

Attempts to enclose the commons have always been characterized by intensive contestation. So it is with the new global enclosures. Whether it is the privatization of public water in Bolivia, the displacement of tens of millions of indigenous people from the land in rural India to make way for transnational mining companies and agribusinesses like Monsanto, or efforts to defund and further privatize secondary and higher education in Santiago, Chicago, or Montreal, the new enclosures have been met by extensive opposition from commoners who have sought to retain democratic control over common resources for collective benefit. There are several overlapping instances of the common inaugurated by globalization that highlight present contestations between forces of enclosure and democratic potentiality. We discuss each of these in turn below.

The Transnational Common

In the first place, globalization results in the weakening of the boundaries between and the reconfiguration of the geography of groupings of people in political, cultural, and economic terms. Politically, the locus of power begins to migrate from national states to supranational and transnational frameworks. At the same time, as capital broadens its reach to absorb new regions and modes of life, the logics of reification, consumerism, and cultural commodification unite diverse populations globally. This is also, however, potentially the occasion for a creative kind of appropriation, as these global cultural and economic logics are differentially negotiated by populations from their own standpoints and for their own purposes, in the context of a dramatically more complex cultural infrastructure of technology and media. At the same time, these transformations influence the possibilities for emancipatory movements. On this terrain, the construction of the common as democratic horizon means creating alliances of workers, oppressed groups, and concerned citizens that do not depend for their coherence on national allegiance and that can develop analyses of exploitation, racism, and patriarchy as transnational processes. A global movement of the common organizes the energy of people everywhere in singular moments of global expression, as in the spectacular transnational protests against the meetings of the World Trade Organization; such expressions exceed the logic of the international and potentially suggest a new global subject of opposition.

The Communicative Common

It can be argued that the most significant development of the global era is the tremendous ramification of networks of communication and information. These transform global politics, capital flows, and the textures of everyday life. This promiscuous web-building binds together the nodes of the collective more powerfully and variously. Hardt and Negri have argued that the inherent creativity of humanity, which Marx identified with the ability to produce value in the labor process, is evident most clearly in this domain of communication and information exchange. They argue that this virtual collaboration and inventiveness represents an "immaterial labor" that capital increasingly attempts to capture and exploit (e.g., in the information technology, advertising, and service industries). A central political task is then to organize the new potentials of global communicative networks for democracy-building movements. In the process, the identity of such movements is transformed, as they are joined within a transnational horizon and contemplate their obstacles at this scale. The horizon of the global, as it becomes accessible to progressive theory and practice, opens up unprecedented possibilities for radical articulations between sites, and thus for new oppositional identifications. In this context, diverse moments of protest are sutured into new popular demands at the transnational scale; these new formations can be seen, for example, in youth uprisings across North Africa and Western Europe, in global women's movements, and in international alliances among peasants, indigenous communities, and environmental action coalitions.

The Postcolonial Common

One important implication of these processes is that global left politics is made complex and decentered; in particular, the Eurocentric determination of critical traditions in theory and practice is challenged in favor of a liberatory understanding based on the profound imbrication of global territories, and on the agency and priority of the global South within this context.[9] The complex recombinations produced by globalization as political economy create new possibilities for oppositional identifications and complex alliances at the same time that new populations are subject to exploitation. For example, the increasing importance of service work within the urban spaces of the global economy, the transnational migrations produced by the demand for cheap labor in this sector, and the recruitment of women in this context create the possibility for a new compound social movement oriented at once to gendered and classed identities.[10] These complexities in the cultural dimensions of work and resistance in the context of globalization point to the complexity of the common itself as a space of combination, intersection, and hybridity. This is not quite the hybridity of a genteel cosmopolitanism, which surveys the panorama of the global from a point above the ordeal of its concrete production, but rather an on-the-ground clash and combination of languages, histories, and struggles—as, for instance, in the powerful remaking of both the US labor movement and working-class culture by immigrants from Mexico and Central America. In this sense, the common is not the gray space of a bland universalism, but is rather *full of its differences*—it is the material and concrete space of the collective making of history.

The Ecological Common

Finally, the proliferation of natural disasters in the context of global climate change, the disappearance of biodiversity as a result of habitat destruction and agricultural monoculture, and the rising challenges of water and food scarcity all point to the historicity of nature itself, as well as to the impossibility of reserving historical and ontological priority for human beings. In the context of this sense of shared time and space, the earth itself can be seen to participate in the kind of subjecthood that has been reserved up to now for human beings. At the same time, the ecological is essentially linked to the economic, both because processes of production and consumption are the material foundation of ecological destruction and because ecology names an analysis of *the dynamics of the whole*, not just of nature by itself.[11] A global-ecological perspective reveals the common *par excellence*: the material body of the totality—the earth itself. This means that a project for a democratic globality has to challenge more than the abstract irrationality of the relations of economic production; it also has to confront the social and environmental violence of globalization. In the moment of ecological crisis, we can begin to see past the veil of reification that captures relations between humans and their surroundings. A deeper conception of the democratic common becomes possible, one that unites efforts to defend the environment with efforts against economic exploitation and political marginalization.

It is important to understand that the common as a political project is always provisional and in process, rather than the mere result of an objective dialectic. The new possibilities for democracy that are proposed in the social and political reconfigurations of the global era emerge as such *against* the ongoing efforts of power to construct global society in its own image; these possibilities constitute an *outside* to the grammar defined by capital's fundamental binding of processes of life, creativity, and construction to the modes of the private and the proprietary. It is important to emphasize that *democracy* itself is an ambiguous signifier. It has often been equated simply with capitalism—the boosters of market-driven globalization consider it to be a natural corollary of economic expansion in the new "flat world."[12] But this framing of democracy, measured by levels of profit-oriented entrepreneurialism and commodity consumption and by a narrow electoral politics and exported to the world under the flag of imperialism, is exactly what the emerging sense of the common we have described above begins to contest. At the same time, then, that we envision an alternative globality directed against the top-down globalization organized by elites, we need to imagine an alternative democracy that refuses the constraints imposed by official discourse and practice. This alternative imagination, in challenging directly the processes of appropriation and enclosure associated with neoliberalism and technocracy, ties democracy to a radically emancipatory widening of the possibilities of the lifeworld itself, rather than limiting it to a modification of the institutions of parliamentary politics.

The basic ontological condition that grounds solidarity in education and elsewhere is the fact of our constitutive involvement or entanglement in each other. That is to say, human selves are always already constitutively traded at the level of being, essentially made out of each other, from the common material of life and sociality. Marxist theory has emphasized this process in its explication of the always collective nature of social production, which sets the terrain of selves. But globalization reveals this condition in new ways: through the new kinds of communication between disparatenesses that it produces, the new mobility and hybridity of populations that it occasions, and the new forms of cultural interpenetration that grow out of it. Becoming conscious of this entanglement means being determined against those social structures and processes that deny it; democratic education and a new common school movement find their meaning and purpose in this context. This means a struggle over teaching and learning, as well as over the different kinds of futures that public schooling can produce. Neoliberal education promises the individual potential inclusion in a shrinking system in which the supreme values are commodity acquisition and the objectification of the self and others. The unlimited growth of this system is despoiling the planet and ensuring diminished political agency to collectively address public problems. In what follows, we appropriate from both the original common school movement in the United States and the recent literature on the commons to suggest another path for schooling in the present.

◆

CHAPTER 3

A Brief History of Educational Conflict

We turn now to charting how the history of US schooling has been shaped by struggles over the educational commons. The institution of modern public education has historically functioned and operated as a contested commons—a publicly managed social resource intimately tied to the production of human capacities and shared potentialities. Perhaps no other institution has more fully embodied both the democratic promise and the injustices inherent to modern life. On the one hand, schooling has always been embedded within the market, property, and power relations immanent to capitalism and its moral economy. While historically understood in liberal and universal terms, schools have played a formative role in sorting young people disadvantaged by class, race, and ethnicity into their "proper places" in the labor and consumer hierarchy. On the other hand, public schools have also historically served as a crucial site in which progressives have struggled to create an opportunity for young people, regardless of their social position, to develop their human potential and intellectual and civic agency in ways that prepare them for social and democratic engagement and ultimately unpredictable futures.

The Original Common School Movement

The US public school system has its origins in the common school movement in Massachusetts under Horace Mann in the nineteenth century. The movement eventually spread throughout the United States. Historical tensions and struggles over public schooling between progressive and conservative commitments were clearly embodied by Mann and within the common school movement itself. From 1837 to 1848, Mann used his position as secretary of the Massachusetts Board of Education to advocate for a universal system of common schools largely as an antidote to the ills associated with capitalist modernization. During this period, mass migration from rural to urban areas, the emergence of industrial production and labor, and a vast influx of European immigrants generated new class tensions and social cleavages. Between 1790 and 1840, the nation's urban population swelled from under 1 million to over 11 million people.[1] In cities like New York, Philadelphia, and Boston, dehumanizing living and working conditions in sprawling new urban slums, tenement houses, and factories inspired significant class resentment.[2] Sometimes, these frustrations were channeled into reactionary movements and hatred toward Catholic, Irish, African American, and Native American individuals and communities. At other times, they inspired working-class solidarity and urban and rural rebellions.[3]

Horace Mann viewed the common school as a site of social reform where emergent class conflicts could be assuaged, diverse immigrant populations could be assimilated, and common values could be developed and inculcated.[4] This perspective contained both progressive and conservative elements. Mann believed common schools could provide a check against the degrading and exploitive conditions and class conflicts inherent to American urbanization and industrialization. "Nothing but universal education," he wrote, "can counter-work this tendency to the domination of capital and the servility of labor."[5] Mann's progressivism was rooted in a biblical notion of property and stewardship. For Mann, all forms of property were seen to have a social and collective moral basis as part of a commonwealth. In his view, *property exceeded private property*. It was something fundamental and universal. According to Mann, "All that we call *property*, all that makes up the valuation or inventory of a nation's capital, was prepared at the creation, and was laid up of old in the capacious store-houses of nature."[6] In Mann's view, property has a *social foundation* and thus society has a claim to *a common portion of all property*. Common schools produce social value beneficial to all. Therefore, they were to be collectively supported and managed through public funding and remain nonsectarian in their content and universal in their mission.

Despite Mann's progressive views on property and social reform, the common school movement was also highly conservative. While Mann believed common schools were sites where social problems could be resolved and democratically mediated, he also believed that they should reproduce the existing order of things. During his time as secretary of the Massachusetts Board, Mann spoke directly to the interests of the wealthy and the powerful. His salary was paid by Edmund Dwight, a wealthy industrialist, and he opposed workers' rights to organize. Mann viewed common schools as a sphere for providing the right moral training for the poor so that they would develop proper respect for authority and the habits and dispositions necessary for the demands of industrial labor. Common schools were to be the "balance wheel of the social machinery," imbued with the capacity to "disarm the poor of their hostility toward the rich" and condition them to accept their "proper" place in the social hierarchy.[7] Furthermore, despite claims to universality, common schools systematically excluded Native Americans, ethnic minorities, and blacks whose very slave labor in the South provided the raw materials for the Northern industrial boom. Thus, the original common school movement, while containing progressive democratic elements, ultimately operated under *a limited conception of the common*. Mann understood the common school as an integral component of a commonwealth. However, this commonwealth was defined not by fundamental equality and democratic possibility but by both formal and informal systems of exclusion and exploitation. The common school was a site framed within an *abstract*, as opposed to a *concrete*, notion of universality while largely legitimating systems of domination. It assumed inequality at the outset and therefore a limited notion of what a common school could be.

Corporate Management, Progressivism, and the Birth of Public Education

These tensions in the original common school movement were reproduced in the early twentieth century with the rise of modern public education. During this period, a new breed of educational managers emerged who not only believed that common schools should function as an adjunct to industry but sought to transform their very organization on the model of the factory and the corporation. The period between 1890 and 1930 was the era of monopoly capitalism embodied by figures like J. P. Morgan, John D. Rockefeller, and Andrew Carnegie. Revolutions in industry, rooted in the "scientific management" principles of Fredrick Winslow Taylor, transformed the corporate firm and factory into large vertically integrated units with multilayered and fine-grained distributions of authority and standardized function.[8] Armed with Taylor's theories of scientific management, educationalists such as Franklin Bobbitt and David Snedden sought to fundamentally retool the educational system in the image of the industrial age. In 1916, Elwood Cubberly, a national education leader, described this vision:

> Our schools are, in a sense, factories in which the raw materials (children) are to be shaped and fashioned into products to meet the various demands of life. The specifications for manufacturing come from the demands of the twentieth century civilization, and it is the business of the school to build its pupils to the specifications laid down. This demands good tools, specialized machinery, continuous measurement of production to see if it is according to specifications, the elimination of waste in manufacture and a large variety of output.[9]

Social efficiency and *utility* became the watchwords of modern public schooling as the use value of education was aimed squarely at the reproduction of exchange value. In a bulletin put out by the High School Teachers Association of New York in 1911, the purpose of scientific management was described as increasing "the efficiency of the laborer, i.e., the pupil"; increasing "the quality of product, i.e., the pupil"; and thereby increasing "the amount of output and the value to the capitalist." The bulletin went on to state that "the teacher obviously corresponds to the manager of a factory" and that "workmen, raw material, and finished product are combined in the pupil."[10]

Such thinking was fundamental in the expansion of large school bureaucracies, vocational and academic tracking, compulsory primary and secondary schools, the introduction of standardized subject areas and testing, and the feminization and standardization of teacher work. Within mass compulsory public schooling, heavy emphasis was placed on drill, routine, control, discipline, standardization, and examination. I.Q. testing, which was based in the overtly racist eugenics movement, served to sort students of different class, gender, and ethnic backgrounds into their preordained place in the industrial hierarchy. Corporate titans like Rockefeller and Carnegie established private foundations that invested millions in such testing services.[11] They looked to the school system to promote their economic interests while stabilizing existing divisions of wealth and power. Despite being couched in the language of civic virtue, the common school was imagined by corporate management largely in functionalist terms—a public mechanism for sorting human capital and subsidizing private gain.

While the influence of business and scientific management significantly impacted the organization of public education in the early twentieth century, pockets of opposition also flourished. This was a time when the democratic philosophy of John Dewey gained prominence and when progressive teachers' unions and progressive professional associations were established. The social progressives viewed the corporate efficiency movement and the influence of business with contempt. In their view, the public schools were not meant to be industrial mills for working up and sorting human capital, but rather sites for human and democratic development. The editors of *American Teacher*, the official journal of the American Federation of Teachers, wrote in 1916:

> If efficiency means the demoralization of the school system; dollars saved and human materials squandered; discontent, drudgery and disillusion—We'll have none of it!

If efficiency denotes low finance, bickering and neglect; exploitation, suspicion and inhumanity; larger class sizes, smaller pay and diminished joy—We'll have none of it![12]

Published in 1916, Dewey's monumental *Democracy and Education* offered a powerful rebuke of corporate management. It positioned the public school as a vehicle for transmitting the values, principles, aspirations, shared concerns, and critical dispositions necessary for the operation of democracy. If corporate administrators viewed education in terms of control and utility, Dewey viewed it as a means to foster social and democratic development and what he referred to as a "common life." It is important to understand that, for Dewey, democracy was conceived not simply as a *passive* schema of voting and representation but rather as an *active* "mode of associated living, of conjoint communicated experience."[13] Without a critical and deliberative *educational commons*, democracy would simply become inoperable.

Influenced by such ideas, public schools became sites of reform and struggle as parents, teachers, and communities often asserted their voice in educational affairs. Teachers' unions like the New York Teachers Union, founded in 1916 and later destroyed by McCarthyism in the 1950s, waged campaigns to fight corporate management and to end poverty and racial discrimination in schools and communities.[14] In the 1930s, the socialist educational theory of George Counts and the reconstructionists experienced a brief but formative popularity. Such movements laid the foundation for later civil rights struggles to abolish racial segregation in the 1950s and to promote decentralization, local control, and other democratic experiments in the 1960s and 1970s. If corporate management framed the value of public schooling in terms of its utility to business and its efficiency in fostering workforce discipline and social control, progressivism established a legacy whereby the value of public schooling was to be measured by its capacity to produce a socially responsive and democratic commons.[15] It is precisely this radical democratic impulse in the progressive tradition that has been abandoned by contemporary liberalism, which allows its analyses and prescriptions to be framed by the terms of the neoliberal consensus; and it is this democratic impulse that we aim here to reinvigorate and develop for the contemporary context.

From Progressive Liberalism to Neoliberal Ascendancy

In the middle decades of the twentieth century, corporate management and progressivism established an uneasy truce. The destabilizing impact of the Great Depression and the horrors of World War II were enough to convince the American elite that a basic social contract was necessary to promote economic reconstruction and to neutralize the growing appeal of socialist and other radical currents in public life.[16] This contributed to elevating the ideas of John Maynard Keynes to prominence in the postwar period and led to the establishment of a *progressive liberal consensus* in public policy. Recognizing that capitalism is by nature a self-destructive and exploitive system, Keynes argued for governmental intervention and public investment, particularly in the sphere of education, to promote economic stability and maintain social consent. Under this system, workers maintained basic rights and wage and benefit guarantees in exchange for their cooperation with management and their rejection of radical demands. This led to an unprecedented economic boom driven by rising wages, the birth of the middle class, and a liberal reformist approach to governance. It also led to an unprecedented expansion of public educational investment in the 1950s and 1960s that created a system of publicly funded and universal secondary and higher education that became the envy of the world.

The period between 1945 and 1975 is often referred to as the "golden age" of US capitalism. However, most of the benefits went to a workforce dominated by white men, and the American system remained entrenched in class, race, and gender hierarchies. Further, despite Dwight D. Eisenhower's prescient warnings, the Cold War provided fertile soil for a blooming corporate-military-industrial complex and with it neo-imperialist adventurism and atrocities in South Asia and Latin America. Long-standing historical frustrations over the failure to realize the democratic ideals that the US political system supposedly represented, and the realities of what

Dr. Martin Luther King Jr. referred to as the "three evils" of poverty, racism, and war, came to a head in the 1960s and early 1970s in a series of demands by women, African Americans, gays and lesbians, and other excluded groups for economic and political justice. The civil rights movement and other social movements of the time culminated in Lyndon Johnson's Great Society, the Civil Rights Act of 1964, and the Elementary and Secondary Education Act of 1965. These measures provided significant federal funding for poverty reduction, job training, and health care for low-income families, as well as for public educational opportunity and access for disadvantaged youth and communities.

Although they extended basic civil rights and access to education and other social benefits, the liberal policies of this era should not be overly romanticized. They often proved obsessively bureaucratic and paternalistic and ultimately never seriously attempted to alter the mechanisms that maintained exclusion and injustice. For instance, educational reforms during the 1960s were predicated on deficit models of racial inequality based on a "culture of poverty" discourse, signified perhaps most famously by Daniel Patrick Moynihan's reference to a "tangle of pathology," which referred to impoverished black families and which tended to reinforce, rather than uproot, racist stereotypes and practices in public schools. Further, public schools, especially those that served poor and working-class youth, too often remained soul-deadening places that reproduced the drudgery and authoritarianism of the industrial workplace. Rather than a means of authentic egalitarian social transformation, schooling was viewed largely as a means to ameliorate the most blatant forms of oppression while stabilizing the hierarchical economic and political divisions within the US system.[17] This being said, however, and contrary to neoconservative assertions regarding the failures of "big government," progressive policies in the 1960s nevertheless led for a short time to the near equalization of school funding between urban and suburban districts, reduced child poverty rates to 60 percent of what they are today, resulted in heavy investment in hiring and retaining high-quality teachers in underserved schools, and led to college enrollment rates for minority youth comparable to those of whites for the only time either before or since.[18]

During this era, public education remained rooted in systems of institutional injustice governed by the imperatives of cultural assimilation and reproduction of the class structure of society. However, it also provided a sphere for human and democratic development. In short, public schooling functioned as *a contested commons* where communities, educators, and students often pushed for reform, equity, and greater social and political inclusion. As John Bellamy Foster notes, while progressive movements and social democratic policy failed historically to displace corporate management or uproot systemic inequalities in public schooling, "they did succeed in keeping education within the public sphere, maintaining basic democratic values, and preserving hope and the possibility of a more egalitarian educational future."[19]

The movement that began under Horace Mann laid the intellectual and organizational foundation for a universal system of publicly managed common schools. It was not until the rise of neoliberal rationality and the neoconservative revolutions under Reagan in the 1980s that this basic understanding of public education began to change. The progressive liberal consensus was gradually reorganized into a neoliberal consensus, which was accompanied by a new regime of reductive corporate management and social exclusion. Many contemporary educational reforms, such as increased reliance on standardized testing, scripted curriculum, and teacher accountability mandates, resemble older factory-based efficiency models championed by early twentieth-century reformers like Elwood Cubberly and Franklin Bobbitt. What makes neoliberal education policies different from this earlier corporate efficiency movement, however, is that not only are they geared toward promoting the forms of management and skills necessary for workforce discipline, which today are described in terms of developing "twenty-first-century skills" and globally competitive "entrepreneurial-citizens," but they also take the market itself as the very basis for educational organization and value. Put differently, they are rooted in the desire to break up what is referred to as the "public school monopoly" through the wholesale *privatization of the educational commons*. In this new schema of corporate management, public schooling is no longer simply viewed as a public mechanism for promoting labor market discipline and social control. In its very structure, it is to be modeled on the principles of market exchange and transformed into a site of economic valorization and expropriation. Understanding this transition and its consequences for considering the future of the educational commons requires delving deeper into the political economy of the neoliberal era and its relationship to educational change.

◊

CHAPTER **4**

The Dual Crisis of Neoliberalism and Progressive Education

Educational enclosure under neoliberalism reflects broader tectonic shifts in global capitalism over the last four decades. The liberal Keynesian consensus that presided over the American postwar economic boom began to fall apart in the mid-1970s. This was because of a deep *structural crisis of profitability* for US capitalism precipitated by a number of intersecting trends: rising wages and growth stagnation (stagflation), powerful labor unions and social democratic checks on corporate power, and spiking energy costs and a dearth of opportunities for the profitable reinvestment of surplus capital. The answer for capital was found in a series of class strategies meant to offset these structural constraints and return the system to profitability and growth. This response was backed by the adoption of neoliberal political rationality under Reagan in the United States and Thatcher in the United Kingdom in the early 1980s. Originally viewed as a marginal economic doctrine confined to quirky Austrian thinkers and neoconservative think tanks, neoliberal ideology soon became the driving intellectual force of the global era, first by discrediting its Keynesian predecessor, and second by working to extend the structural and cultural logic of the commodity-form to every aspect of late modern life. After the fall of the Soviet Union and "actually existing socialism" in 1989, Margaret Thatcher's famous dictum that "there is no alternative" was broadly enshrined as the accepted wisdom.

32

Armed with market fundamentalism, globalization opened new territories for capitalist expansion principally by breaking down nationstate and international barriers to the global mobility of production and capital and incorporating vast new reserves of workers across Asia and the global South. This enabled capital to drive down wages through union busting, outsourcing, automation, and temporary "flexible" contracting. Alongside these processes, neoliberal state restructuring made possible a new round of enclosures of the global commons through the widespread defunding and privatization of health and education systems, utilities, transportation, communications, land, and natural resources. These strategies restored profitability in the 1980s and 1990s by lowering wages in the core countries and lowering barriers to the expansion of capital across global space and time. They have also contributed to extensive *uneven development* that has generated historic concentrations of wealth and power at the top of the global class structure and a deepening chasm of social inequality across the global division of labor. (Today, the richest fifty individuals in the world have a combined income greater than the poorest 416 million; 2.5 billion people—or 40 percent of the world's population—live on less than $2 a day, while 54 percent of global income goes to the richest 10 percent of the world's population.)[1]

Globalization and neoliberal restructuring may have provided a short-term fix for the crisis of the 1970s, but in the process, they have created new systemic instabilities. In the United States and other developed nations, we have witnessed record-breaking corporate profits and vast elite wealth accumulation. However, since the 1980s, we have also seen dramatic social polarization, inequality, and the erosion of working-class livelihoods. This has generated problems related to *effective demand*—the capacity of consumers to purchase goods and services and therefore support economic growth. This problem was temporarily mitigated by the vast expansion of easy credit, consumer debt, and finance capital in the 1990s and early 2000s. But this reliance on "fictitious" capital to boost growth and consumption met the hard realities of the "real" economy in 2008 with the collapse of Wall Street and the ensuing global financial crisis. David McNally observes:

The Great Recession of 2008–9 represents a profound rupture in the neoliberal era, signaling the exhaustion of the accumulation regime that had emerged almost thirty years earlier. Rather than an ordinary recession, a short-lived downturn in the business cycle, it constituted a systemic crisis, a major contraction whose effects will be with us for many years to come. Among those effects are the extraordinary cuts to social programs, and the resultant impoverishment, announced as part of the Age of Austerity inaugurated by all major states.[2]

As McNally and other analysts have noted, austerity is a strategic response by transnational capital markets, financial elites, and institutions to discipline nation-states to socialize the costs of the global economic crisis. Concretely, this means that the toxic debt that accumulated in the banking and financial system originating from the US subprime housing and securities markets has been converted into sovereign debt through massive government bailouts. Rather than punishing those financial institutions whose excesses tanked the global economy, the costs, along with future financial risks, are being passed along to the public and to the poor through the intensification of neoliberal privatization, painful cuts to social services, and continued tax breaks for corporations and the rich. What we have seen are spiraling levels of social inequality and insecurity: mass foreclosures; evaporating wages and savings; levels of unemployment, homelessness, and poverty not seen since the Great Depression; and an explosion of personal bankruptcy and debt.

In the United States, austerity reflects commitments to the same failed supply-side, trickle-down economics embraced under Reagan in the 1980s. Painfully demonstrative of what happens to a society when unfettered capitalism is mindlessly conflated with democracy, the United States now stands as the most unequal advanced nation, with relative levels of social inequality comparable to many of the poorest nations in Africa and Latin America. Despite three decades of economic growth (90 percent of which went to the top 10 percent) and despite record-breaking corporate profits in the post-2008 period (95 percent of which have accrued mainly to the top 1 percent), 97.3 million Americans are now defined as "low-income" or "near poverty" largely because of declining wages, reduced hours, job losses, and rising costs of living, while an additional 49 million struggle to survive below the federal poverty line.[3] Meanwhile, the United States continues to pour trillions of dollars into supporting the planet's largest and most costly military and prison industrial complexes. According to the Pew Research Center, in the nation that brands itself as a global beacon of freedom and justice, one in thirty-one adults are currently under the direct control of the criminal justice system (either in prison, on parole, or on probation).[4] The trend toward mass incarceration of the poor and dispossessed, combined with seemingly limitless investments in militarism and warfare, has exposed new affinities between free-market governance and authoritarian power. As a point of comparison, total spending on defense and homeland security in the United States in 2013 is slated to be roughly $1 trillion, while federal investment in education in 2013 is expected to be only $64 billion.[5] What has emerged in the United States over this period is a hyperfragmented and punitive society—a society in which corporate forces and a fanatic right wing stand determined to roll back all vestiges of social progress made in the previous century.

Within this milieu, a turn to punishment has become a central feature of neoliberal governance. It is part of a broader reorientation of the state in which it reduces its commitment to a social safety net in favor of an emphasis on disciplining the poor. Today, the United States has 5 percent of the world's population but warehouses 25 percent of the world's prison inmates. The turn to punishment reveals the racial logic of neoliberalism, since people of color are disproportionately the targets of the criminal justice system; recent data show, for instance, that African Americans are incarcerated at a rate more than six times that of whites, most for nonviolent drug offenses, even though African Americans make up only 13 percent of the population and a small fraction of illegal drug users.[6] Ruth Gilmore demonstrates that the development of this racialized regime of punishment takes place in response to a set of political-economic crises in which the state has to manage surpluses of capital, land, and black and brown bodies. As living-wage employment has disappeared, and economic valorization has become increasingly global and dependent on precarious service work and finance, large segments of the population have become functionally redundant to the system. Rather than imagined as needing or deserving investment for the future, they are conceived as excess or surplus populations.[7] In this way, the growth of the prison system under neoliberalism is simultaneously an economic and racial project. Furthermore, the carceral turn in the present continues a historic legacy of excessive punishment of people of color in the United States. In particular, the experience of African Americans can be understood in terms of a persistent condition of confinement and control, from slavery to the convict-lease system to the modern prison-industrial complex.[8] The neoliberal prison system builds on and multiplies this condition, and in this context, the contemporary turn to punishment is simultaneously a strategy for managing surplus extraction and a racialized instrument of social and political repression.

The combination of austerity, escalating inequality, and surplus repression is not only toxic to human dignity and the social fabric but also bad for a capitalist economy—widespread loss of jobs and low wages for workers stifle demand for goods and services, while decaying public infrastructure and frayed safety nets erode traditional means of domestic economic development. However, we must understand that rising inequality and the degradation of the public are only considered a problem from the standpoint of US capital if we assume that the corporate and political elite still require a strong middle class and the public and social infrastructures necessary to support one. As it has gone global, US capital is less reliant on domestic labor, and elites are less inclined to view social and public investments as necessary. The elite now rely on private services, private education, private health care, and private investment–related retirement and social security. And they believe everyone else should as well, particularly as this generalized privatization represents a source of profit. As Maurizio Lazzarato has observed, this means a life of insecurity and debt for the majority. No job or living wage—here is a line of consumer credit with interest. No public tuition—here are educational loans with interest. Instead of public retirement benefits, here is a personal savings account tied to the too-big-to-fail casino. Instead of public health care, here are private market exchanges and private insurance. When you are unable to afford health insurance or to pay back your medical bills, here is a for-profit debtor's prison.[9]

What we have seen is *a privatization of social reproduction itself*—that is, a privatization of the innumerable ways in which we reproduce the conditions of our lives and collective livelihoods. This has contributed not only to the defunding of the public through austerity but also to a *pillaging* of the public and the institutional structures of social reproduction through their enclosure for private wealth and profit. In the context of education, this has involved, among other things, the replacement of public schools in working-class and poor communities with charter contracts, voucher schemes, and scholarship tax credits to induce parents to opt out of the public system. As we detail below, school privatizations in the United States stand to capture roughly $600 billion per year in public tax wealth, for instance by underpaying teachers through chartering and de-unionization. The longer-term neoliberal project involves establishing a system of "churn" or "creative destruction" to naturalize private contracting and to eliminate the public infrastructure for public schools. The rapidly growing for-profit prison industry is an important parallel to the pillage economics of neoliberal educational restructuring. Poor students rendered economically disposable and redundant in an economy with too little upward mobility and too few jobs can become, as in prisons, the basis for investor profit simply by being in schools. Each student represents a commodity to investors between per pupil public tax spending and expenditures on teacher pay and overhead.

Marx pointed out that history has a tendency to happen "behind the backs" of not only workers but capitalists as well. The hollowing out of the public and the privatization of social reproduction threaten economic expansion as austerity erodes the collective basis of capitalist wealth by generating savage inequalities and diminishing the general intellect and the lives and purchasing power of workers. This process also contributes to the problem of *overaccumulation*, whereby there is more global productive capacity and excess capital than there are avenues for profitable reinvestment. We can see this in the fact that US corporations are currently sitting on trillions in capital reserves with seemingly few avenues to profitably reinvest them domestically. For a while, neoliberalism was able to overcome these problems through wage repression, corporate and elite tax cut stimulus, new credit and debt arrangements, financial innovations, bailouts, speculative manipulation, and the privatization of the commons itself. However, the ongoing financial crisis that began in 2008 has revealed new limits in a global system loaded with toxic debt, limited avenues to expand and invest world output, and looming ecological exhaustion.

What we have seen is the global discrediting of neoliberal ideology as a viable long-term strategy for capital accumulation. In some corners, against all evidence, this has led to a doubling down on market fundamentalism. (In the United States, we are incessantly told that more austerity and further upward distribution of wealth to the "job creators" will magically solve the very problems that they create.) The *failure of neoliberalism* has also simultaneously contributed to the emergence of varied discourses on the importance of rethinking the relationship between *capitalism* and *the commons*. On the one hand, there is a renewed interest in the commons among global development planners and policy analysts at the United Nations and World Bank as well as among certain sectors of the global business class itself. There is a growing understanding that radical deregulation and extension of unfettered market forces into every aspect of existence produce social and environmental externalities that are toxic to the long-term interests of capital accumulation. As Silvia Federici sardonically puts it in relation to the "new commons" and "business commons" rhetoric now circulating among the elite, "capital is now learning the virtues of the common good."[10] On the other hand, while some sectors of the global technocratic and business class are rediscovering the benefits of the commons as a means *to save capitalism from itself*, there is also a growing recognition that an *endless-growth political economy is fundamentally irrational and unsustainable* on a planet with finite resources. Certainly, this sentiment can be found among a new generation of global social movements that have called for an end to corporate and state exploitation of people and the environment and a renewed commitment to rethinking the global commons for a sustainable future. However, the question that concerns us at the moment is, what does all of this have to do with public schooling? We suggest below that the contemporary crisis in the meaning and purpose of educational reform is the first aspect of a "dual crisis" that schooling reveals in the present; the other side of this dual crisis is the deep political-economic crisis itself that neoliberalism attempts to overcome, including in its reshaping of education.[11]

Educational Enclosure and the Dual Crisis

As we have suggested, the history of US public schooling has always been defined by a struggle over the value and organization of the educational commons. This has involved tensions between conservative and progressive forces that have sought to alter public education according to divergent agendas. These struggles were embodied in the original common school movement in Horace Mann's social democratic views on property combined with his commitment to social control within a fundamentally unequal and exploitive industrial order. These tensions were reproduced in the twentieth century with the birth of corporate management and progressivism in modern public education. The former viewed schooling in terms of maximizing economic utility and subsidizing private industry, while the latter dreamed of an educational system oriented to full human development and egalitarian democracy. Although progressivism has had a lasting impact on educational theory and influenced educational reform in the 1960s and 1970s, it was ultimately unsuccessful in uprooting reductive corporate management and injustice in the practice and structure of schooling and never seriously attempted to challenge the hierarchical race and class structure of US capitalism. These struggles have been recast in the contemporary era.

The economic crisis of the 1970s and the transition to neoliberal and neoconservative governance in the 1980s had a significant impact on public schooling. During this time, poverty and inequality began to steadily increase in the United States at the same time that federal, state, and local investment in public education began to dramatically decline. As Bellamy Foster observes, the Reagan administration was responsible for cutting taxes on the rich and corporations and pouring money into a Cold War military buildup, all while slashing funds for public education at all levels, including a 50 percent cut in Title 1 funds to low-income schools. The deterioration of communities stemming from deindustrialization, stagnating wages, and declining state and local revenue and educational investment contributed to the erosion of the gains in educational achievement, equity, and access that had been achieved during the 1960s and early 1970s, particularly in the historically most disadvantaged and vulnerable neighborhoods and schools. In 1983, the Reagan administration presided over a national commission on education and the release of a report entitled *A Nation at Risk.* The report famously described the state of the nation's public schools in military terms: "If an unfriendly foreign power had attempted to impose on America the mediocre educational performance that exists today, we might well have viewed it as an act of war." The report fueled the perception that public education was failing not because of economic hardship, poverty, or institutional neglect but because of a lack of competition and corporate oversight. Inspired by the exuberant ideological climate that accompanied the end of the Cold War and the emergence of the much hyped "end of history" supposedly inaugurated by neoliberal globalization, formerly fringe notions that public schools should be exposed to market forces and run like businesses suddenly became mainstream talking points of the political elite in the 1990s and 2000s. This created a cultural opening for a new corporate reform movement and for calls to expose US public schools to market competition, choice, testing, teacher discipline, and extensive privatization.

The market ethos has since become a broadly shared form of "common sense" among the elite. It has been pushed by both major political parties; an extensive network of well-funded neoliberal and neoconservative think tanks like the Heritage Foundation and the Fordham and Hoover institutes; corporate philanthropic organizations like the Bill and Melinda Gates, Broad, Dell, and Walton Family foundations; business groups like the Business Roundtable and Chamber of Commerce; and corporate media, such as recent films like *Waiting for "Superman"* and *The Lottery.* The adoption of neoliberal policy has promoted the wholesale enclosure of the educational commons. The stated aims of the corporate reform alliance have been to support privatization and school commercialism, to advance the dismantling of teachers' unions, and to impose a system of corporate management and market discipline on public schools. In terms of policy, this has meant the promotion of market-based choice initiatives and the proliferation of publicly funded but privately run charter and contract schools, as well as direct for-profit secondary education. It has also meant efforts to bring market-based strategies of accountability and institutional "efficiency" modeled on the corporation into schooling at all levels—particularly through standardization, auditing and accountability mechanisms, and emphasis on the rote learning of "basic skills" combined with mandatory high-stakes testing. These reform strategies were codified into law with the passage of George W. Bush's No Child Left Behind legislation in 2001 and have continued under the Obama administration through policies like Race to the Top.

At all levels of educational endeavor, these policy architectures have sought to convert schooling into a marketplace, to subordinate educational value to economic value, and to open all facets of education to profit-making and to the logic of corporate culture. These processes have only intensified in the post-2008 period of economic decline and generalized social insecurity and austerity. We suggest that current attempts to enclose the educational commons represent a "dual crisis" of neoliberal political economy and culture as they intersect with the collapse of progressive education. This dual crisis can be understood through several interlinking processes, described below.

1. Strategic Devaluation

Educational enclosure has been lubricated by *the strategic devaluation* of certain sectors of the public educational system, particularly in poor and dispossessed communities, through state-to-market transfers of public money. For instance, a 2011 report by the National Education Association titled *Starving America's Public Schools* details how the spiraling costs of the Great Recession are currently being passed along to schools and communities through further cutbacks and disinvestment.[12] Since 2008, states have laid off hundreds of thousands of teachers and staff, cut back curriculum and extracurricular programs, expanded class sizes, shortened school days and weeks, and even closed many schools altogether. For example, Illinois has cut $152 million, New York $1.3 billion, Pennsylvania $422 million,

Washington $1 billion, and Arizona $560 million in state funding to K–12 public schools, early childhood education, and child development services. Further, the report details that while educational budgets are being slashed, public money that would be going directly to schools is instead being redirected to corporate vendors mainly for expanding privatized commercial management, for-profit commercial curriculum contracts, for-profit commercial online "cyber-charter" school ventures, and for-profit commercial standardized testing services (a booming aspect of the $600-billion-per-year education market). Florida, as just one example, has cut $1 billion from its educational budget while redirecting roughly $299 million to corporate interests in the education market. These cuts are contributing to the erosion of the human development mission of public schools by raising class sizes, narrowing curriculum, and eliminating essential services, particularly in the poorest communities, while redirecting funds from the public to private interests (corporate lobbying for vast educational contracts has become a grand enterprise in the post–No Child Left Behind era). These extensive cutbacks and corporate giveaways legitimate further privatization by inhibiting the capacity of public schools to meaningfully serve their students.

2. Structural Privatization

The strategic devaluation of public schools and efforts to capitalize on the educational market have occurred side by side with the *structural privatization* of the public educational commons. This has meant closing public schools and creating networks of charter, contract, and for-profit schools. Here, schools are imagined as enterprises that need to be managed as businesses that compete against one another for students and resources. In this schema, public schools are transferred over to corporate management, and school systems are converted into a marketplace where parents are charged with "shopping" around for seats. As Naomi Klein has pointed out, the strategic devaluing of the public sector presents businesses with opportunities to institute reforms that enable the transfer of public resources like schools from the public trust to private interests. In the wake of Hurricane Katrina, for instance, market reformers presented the storm as a "golden opportunity" to "clean the slate" and to privatize the historically neglected New Orleans public schools—today 60 percent of New Orleans youth attend charter schools run largely by corporate educational management companies.[13] Numerous projects across North American cities such as New York, Chicago, Philadelphia, Houston, and many others have seized on decades of neglect to privatize segments of the public educational system alongside various other public resources. This process is creating a stark imbalance between public and private wealth and power.

3. Market Management

Structural privatization has also entailed the development of systems of *market management* that have sought to enclose processes of teaching and learning. The new corporate management culture is sometimes referred to as the "new managerialism" or even in slightly more Orwellian terms as "total quality management." It works to legitimate itself largely through promises of less regulation, greater accountability and flexibility, and an end to the bureaucratic inefficiencies of the Keynesian welfare state. Within the context of school organization and curriculum, the new managerialism has led to the proliferation of measurement and outcomes-based practices, such as standardized curriculum, scripted lessons, high-stakes testing, and value-added assessments. Efforts to "teacher proof" the curriculum through scripted programs designed by corporations and contracted to districts, and through value-added strategies that hold teachers accountable directly for student test scores, are held up as objective and supposedly progressive responses to long-standing educational failures. Standards, numbers, and measurable targets do not lie, nor do they have an agenda—so the popular wisdom goes. Additionally, holding teachers responsible for outcomes like meeting test score benchmarks would appear on the surface to promote professional conduct, raise expectations, and ensure accountability. However, neoliberal managerial cultures in education do not lessen regulatory authority and bureaucracy but vastly extend their scope through new systems of surveillance and control. As such, these cultures are representative of what Mark Fisher evocatively refers to as "market Stalinism"—the subordination of all values to measurable cost/benefit calculations and the placing of emphasis on quantifiable "representations of learning" with little concern for their ethical content.[14] This reduces curriculum and teaching to a set of anti-intellectual and individualized procedural skills that sap the imaginative potential and the cooperative power of learning.

4. Profiteering

Each of these strategies of enclosure has opened up new opportunities for converting the educational commons into a site of private wealth and profit. The leaders of the educational enclosure movement include venture philanthropists, Wall Street financiers, hedge fund managers, opportunistic politicians, and corporate CEOs. This corporate reform alliance has used the altruistic language of educational reform and equity to garner widespread support for the cause of privatization. It has also used bare-knuckle politics and corporate lobbying to push states to enact legislation based on nonexistent or dubious research that has worked to erode commitments to traditional public schools while funneling billions of public dollars into the hands of software and online learning companies; educational management organizations and charter operators; consulting and curriculum businesses; and for-profit testing, tutoring, and test preparation service corporations. Consider that *Harper's Magazine* reported that, in 2007, $78 billion in venture capital was invested in US educational start-ups. In 2011, those investments had reached a staggering $452 billion.[15] Wall Street has projected that in just the K–12 online learning market alone, profits are expected to soar 43 percent by 2015 as states are being coerced into lifting the cap on cyber-charter schools, allowing public money that would be going to public schools to instead go to deregulated corporate online learning mills.[16] Major Wall Street firms like Goldman Sachs and Merrill Lynch, alongside major hedge funds and wealth management groups, have all jumped into the K–12 education market, which is estimated to rival the health care market at $600 billion per year. Rob Lytle of the Parthenon Group, a Boston-based consulting firm, has stated that we are starting to "see entire ecosystems of investment opportunity lining up" and that "it could get really, really big."[17] The movement is aware that there is potential for a significant backlash against subordinating the public education system to the logic of profit. CEO of Charter Schools USA Jonathon Hage has compared the for-profit movement to war. He has said that there is an "air game" and a "ground game" against the teachers' unions and other resistant elements and that "investors are going to have to support" candidates and policies that "push back against the push back."[18]

5. Privatizing Responsibility

The enclosure of the educational commons represents the privatization of responsibility. Today, in the wake of the global financial crisis, the United States has one of the highest rates of child poverty, ranking ahead of only Romania on a scale of thirty-five developed nations. Children under eighteen are the largest group living in poverty in the United States.[19] Fifteen million, or 21 percent, of US children live in poverty (nearly double what it was twenty-five years ago), while 31 million, or 42 percent, of all children, now live at the edge of the federal poverty rate ($22,500 a year for a family of four).[20] Slipping into poverty even for a brief period of time has been shown to impede the educational, health, and social development of young people. Furthermore, the United States maintains one of the worst records of advanced nations in providing health and human services to communities, women with children, and early childhood education while maintaining shameful inequalities in educational investment, with a ten-to-one funding ratio between rich and poor districts in some parts of the country. This reinforces a highly unequal and racially segregated system. Thus, rather than working to improve the overall quality of public education within universal norms and a sense of social and collective responsibility, neoliberal systems privatize social problems and responsibility for educational development. They do so by encouraging school choice arrangements and educational markets that position families as consumers and schools as commercial entities required to compete over students and scarce resources. Child poverty, homelessness, home and neighborhood instability, and racism are viewed as private problems, while low educational performance is blamed on supposedly incompetent teachers and their unions. Instead of attempting to address the structural class disparities and social disadvantages that have been proven to shape educational outcomes in struggling schools through common social investment and cooperation with communities and educators, neoliberal reforms favor "get tough" disciplinary systems of control designed to hold schools, teachers, and students accountable for test scores while opening up the system for private profitability.

6. Enclosing Educational Subjects

Importantly, these material and symbolic relations of enclosure need to be understood as attempting to call into being an idealized neoliberal subject of education. This is a subject who largely identifies as a consuming economic actor in a competitive and fragmented environment. It is also a subject who is made morally culpable for his or her own well-being and security regardless of the social and economic circumstances. For the poor, then, and especially for people of color, the ideal neoliberal subject is a *punished* subject, alternately assimilated into and expelled from organized social and economic life. The ideal subject of neoliberal education is one who makes rationally calculated choices in an educational market to acquire scarce educational resources and out-hustle rivals for credentials in an increasingly transient and precarious employment structure. The ideal subject of neoliberal education is one who successfully manages his or her own individual risk by viewing education as an economic instrumentality rather than as a social force for democratic possibility. The ideal subject of neoliberal education is one who is self-identifying rather than one who identifies his or her interests with the fate of the commons or one who attempts to challenge established social relations in common cause with others. The ideal subject of neoliberal education is one with an enclosed imagination and one who is alienated from the commons.

New Enclosures/New Possibilities

The problems and contradictions associated with these various aspects of educational enclosure have been described by extensive social science research over the last decade and are far too vast to detail here. The important thing to point out is that school privatization and neoliberal management have proven to be a colossal failure both in terms of progressive and critical ideals and in the terms set forth by the movement itself. Major studies by Stanford University, University of Colorado, the Economic Policy Institute, and dozens more have concluded that, on average, charter schools and other contract schools perform either worse or no better than traditional public schools; privatization arrangements have tended to further stratify educational systems by defunding traditional public schools and creating tiered options and further inequality in districts; high-stakes standardized testing does not effectively measure the full range of student learning, while it erodes creative teaching and learning; value-added and other accountability schemes do not improve teaching or student outcomes; and the integration of the logic of profit into education has led to incidents of blatant profiteering, mismanagement, and endemic corruption.[21] These problems all point to important inflection points and fissures for challenging neoliberal schooling. The overwhelming failure of the educational enclosure movement only reinforces the need for an educational commons rooted in the values of collective benefit and cooperation in opposition to the reductive logic of market competition and private gain. The former recognizes our intrinsic commonality and equality—our global interdependency. The latter reproduces what Massimo De Angelis refers to as "the hierarchies of power at the center of today's crisis that rank the value of lives, livelihoods and dignities in terms of money."[22]

The enclosure of the educational commons represents a dual crisis of neoliberalism and the progressive project of public education. Consider that the Bureau of Labor Statistics reports that twenty-two out of the top thirty fastest-growing occupations over the next three decades will be in "low wage" and "very low wage" labor niches.[23] The point is that a public educational system that supports a broad middle class is no longer essential for the economic and political elite. Within a context of mounting constraints to endless global capitalist expansion and a global race to the bottom of labor and livelihoods, US schooling need only produce a small number of highly skilled elite professionals, a declining tier of readily exploitable middle managers, and a vast pool of disciplined rudimentary laborers to provide services. Emphasis on standardization, testing, and rote learning of basic skills for the majority makes sense from this perspective, as does the further expropriation of private wealth from the educational commons.

The radical progressive educational tradition as it existed in the original common school movement and throughout the twentieth century is dead. To make such a statement does not mean that there is an absence of opposition to educational enclosure. On the contrary, scores of educators, parents, students, academics, and community activists are openly opposed to corporate management and market experimentation in education and yearn for public schools responsive to the complex needs and desires of youth and their communities; schools that do not reduce learning to issues of market competition, punishment, and test scores; and schools designed to cultivate restorative and sustainable futures for all young people. However, to suggest that the enclosure of the educational commons represents the collapse of the progressive project of education is to face the reality that the forces of privatization and expropriation have gotten the upper hand. Crucially, it is also to suggest that, amid the present crisis of neoliberal capitalism and culture, there is no going back to some mythical golden age of liberal education that was always, in reality, riven by deep structural contradictions and institutional exclusions. The systemic threats to our shared livelihoods that we confront today require new approaches that can revive and reimagine an educational commons to meet the overlapping crises of the twenty-first century. It is to this challenge that we now turn.

◆

CHAPTER 5

Commoning Public Education

As we have described, neoliberalism seeks to assimilate diverse spheres of social activity into the market, in both ideological and material terms. In education, it finds both an untapped terrain of potential surplus production and a crucial site for a broader ideological offensive on behalf of the market and the reconfiguration of social life in terms of individualism, competition, and commodification that capitalism aggressively undertakes in the present. Education is a crucial site of contest in a broader struggle over the meaning of democracy and the organization of the economy. However, it is important to see that the crisis and transformation we are living in the present are also existential ones, as familiar frames for understanding ourselves, our relationships with others, and the communities we are part of are variously challenged and recomposed.

In his essay "The Future of the Commons," David Harvey suggests that the common as a form of collective activity must ground collective rather than individualized property rights and result in collective control over the production process.[1] Public schools are not simply commonly held property. The collective labor of teachers, administrators, and staff comprises the common of the public schools as well. As Harvey explains,

> the collective laboring that is now productive of value must ground collective, not individual, property rights. Value,

49

socially necessary labor time, is the capitalist common, and it
is represented by money, the universal equivalency by which
common wealth is measured. The common is not, therefore,
something extant once upon a time that has since been lost,
but something that, like the urban commons, is continuously
being produced. The problem is that it is just as continuously
being enclosed and appropriated by capital in its commodified
and monetary form.[2]

Neoliberal schooling does just this. It encloses and appro-
priates for capital the collective *labor* of teachers, administrators, staff, and students. And it does so by using public
financing for privatizing public schooling. As real estate
schemes by charters and the vast array of contracting deals
demonstrate, neoliberal schooling also encloses the collective
property of the public school. In some cases, the actual public
school building is given to a private entity such as a charter
school. More frequently, the contracting arrangements that
districts make with for-profit firms result in the extraction
of surplus wealth, most often by decreasing teacher pay and
skimming off profit by contractors. For Harvey, the problem
of the commons is that unregulated individualized capital
accumulation threatens to destroy the laborer and the land,
which are the two basic common property resources. For
example, unregulated individualized capital accumulation
diminishes the teacher's labor by transforming her/his work
from having the potential to be intellectual, civically engaged,
and dialogic and to foster curiosity, questioning, and dissent
into being anti-intellectual, depoliticized, dogmatic, trans-
missional, curiosity-deadening, and creativity-stifling. In
the process, neoliberal schooling erodes not only the public
and civic dimensions of schooling but also schooling as an
economic and productive force. Unregulated individualized
capital accumulation also erodes the potential productivity
of the student's future economic labor by undermining the
creative and cooperative substance of education. The over-
emphasis on standardized testing and curriculum devalues
the teacher's engagement with the specific context and experience of the student and, in doing so, places limitations on
the ability of teaching to produce the kind of subject who
would engage in collective production. Neoliberal schooling

transforms the student's relationship both to creative activity and to time.

The promise of neoliberal schooling for its proponents is that it increases the efficiency of the teacher-laborer through the enforcement of discipline (tighter controls over time, subject matter, and pedagogical methods) and that such efficiency increases the delivery of knowledge to the student-consumer, increasing in turn the potential economic efficiency of the future student-worker. The promise is false at every point. Chartering, for example, which has become captured by a corporate logic and much of which exists for profit extraction, aims to replicate and scale up the most efficient delivery models, extend the teacher day, pay the teacher less, burn out the teacher, and turn over the teacher workforce. All of these are proven effects of chartering, and there is no doubt that these are good means of maximizing short-term profit for educational management companies and other contractors. Importantly, the problem is not only that these destructive reforms are bad for test-based student achievement (which they are).[3] More significantly, these are means of diminishing the creative, intellectual, curiosity-fostering, and critically engaged qualities of teaching and also of devaluing the future productive force of students' labor.[4]

Controlled, rigid, and anti-critical teaching results not in students with a greater capacity for economic productivity but in the opposite. If the goal is to produce docile, disciplined low-skill workers or marginalized people who are excluded from the economy altogether, then these corporate school reforms are right on target. However, ethics and politics aside, this is *short-sighted as an economic strategy* if, as the corporate school reformers allege, the aim of public schooling is to produce future high-tech workers with knowledge of math and science and the creativity to create new projects and new value. The dominant justification for corporate school reform is that it will allow the United States to develop its labor capacity in the high-technology arena toward the end of winning global economic competition. Usually, proponents of the dominant justification call for encouraging students to develop their capacities for entrepreneurialism. It is difficult to see how eroding the capacity of teacher labor to inspire vigorous, creative thinking and intellectual curiosity could contribute to such a capitalist goal. The point not to be missed here is that *even on its own bad terms* of education for capitalist accumulation, *corporate school reform undermines its own aims.* Enclosure of the public school through privatization does create short-term profit, but it destroys the labor and resources of the public school—that is, it destroys its value by expropriating it as productive force.

The task ahead is to imagine pedagogical practices, curriculum, and school organization that enact the global commons. What path should teachers and students take together with communities in recovering control over the work of teaching and learning? How can the struggle against neoliberal school reform not only demand limits on testing and a cessation to privatization in all its guises but also demand that public education be the basis for reimagining the economy in truly democratic form, reimagining the political system and political action not beholden to corporate power and the empty spectacle of commercialized elections, and reimagining human development and culture in terms of public value rather than private benefit? To begin, it is important to note that a new common school movement has an inevitably hopeful dimension to it. The common can be built and expanded, and it can never be fully enclosed because there are parts of human experience that cannot be turned into property and have to be held in common. Compassion, ideas, social relationships, and the planet itself must be held in common. If we consider neoliberal schooling in terms of the commons, we can formulate a response that recognizes both the need for alternative public educational reform and how such reform connects with and furthers possibilities for broader social transformation and the enactment of the global commons for collective benefit.

Toward a New Common School Movement

In perhaps the most widely discussed instantiation of the concept, Michael Hardt and Antonio Negri offer an image of the common that transcends the private sphere, which they associate with capital, and the public sphere, which they associate with the state. For Hardt and Negri, the common, particularly as manifested in cultural production, holds the potential for the development of a true direct democracy beyond capital and the state based on the horizontal and immanent communicative circuits of what they refer to as the "global multitude."[5] Hardt and Negri's project represents an important contribution to the utopian imagination in a moment of its historical enclosure. However, David Harvey has leveled a number of criticisms of Hardt and Negri that we find persuasive, particularly regarding their lack of adequate engagement with the material and logistical basis of politics and social organization. He states that "the presumption that the world's six and a half billion people can be fed, warmed, clothed, housed, and cleaned without any hierarchical form of governance and outside the reach of monetization and markets is dubious in the extreme."[6]

Harvey argues that the potentiality of the common as a political and organizational force requires us to think about new forms of governmental and institutional arrangements. New horizontal and associational configurations offer democratic potential for social movements and also the management of common resources and human relations on a local level. However, our historical moment requires new state and global forms of governance and solidarity to effectively deal with *global problems*, such as nuclear proliferation and climate change, that impact and erode the planetary commons. With this being said, for Harvey the central problematic concerning the commons today is not really about governmental and political organization per se. In fact, he suggests that such discussions tend to obscure debate over more fundamental issues concerning economic production, distribution, and exchange. Today, efforts by capital to expropriate value from common land, labor, and intellect are eroding the well-being and livelihoods of workers in a deregulated race to the bottom, undermining the efficacy of knowledge, and even threatening the very ecological web and texture of life on the planet through impending ecological exhaustion. Harvey suggests that the erosion of the commons globally can only be contained through the "socialization of surplus production and distribution and the establishment of a new common wealth open to all."[7]

What this means for Harvey is that the particulars of institutional arrangements (including public and private) are not the most important concerns when contemplating the common as a political concept and organizational force. Rather, what matters is to rethink *collective labor* for *common benefit.*

> What matters here is not the particular mix of institutional arrangements—enclosures here, extensions of a variety of collective and common property arrangements there—but that the unified effect address the spiraling degradation of common labor and common land resources (including the resources embedded in the "second nature" of the built environment) at the hands of capital. In this effort, the "rich mix of instrumentalities" ... not only public and private but also collective and associational, nested hierarchical and horizontal, exclusionary and open—will all have a key role to play in finding ways to organize production, distribution, exchange, and consumption to meet human needs. The point is not to fulfill the requirements of accumulation for accumulation's sake on the part of the class that appropriates the common wealth from the class that produces it. The point, rather, is to change all that and to find creative ways to use the powers of collective labor for the common good.[8]

One of the issues at stake here is the question of whether the public/private distinction for schooling matters once the aim is established as collective labor for common benefit. While Hardt and Negri reject the public/private split to frame an image of the common based on the immanent capacities of the multitude, Harvey suggests that the public and the private must be part of a broader set of institutional arrangements (including horizontal and communicative ones) that harness the global commons of land and labor in the service of creating more sustainable and democratic economic and ecological relationships. From our perspective, it is necessary to hold on to the public/private division when considering public schooling as a common property resource and to embrace Harvey's insistence on rethinking our institutional arrangements in relation to new forms of democratic governance at multiple scales to reimagine common labor for collective benefit. Our call for a new common school movement recognizes the need to defend and transform the public dimensions of public schooling against private expropriation and control. We further suggest that a new common school movement is oriented to enlarging the public and public schooling in the service of imagining and enacting new formations of the global commons.

In what follows, we provide a series of broad proposals for orienting a new common school movement. We do so with the understanding that these principles are starting points for a larger conversation, because the educational commons is something that can only be made and remade through collective social action. It is important to note, however, that these proposals, while remaining open and somewhat provisional, do not reject political division—in fact, they presuppose it. Educational politics always involves cultural struggles and decisions over values and the distribution of rights and management of resources. Some individuals and communities understand their interests in reactionary ways that view society and the natural world through a lens of religious fundamentalism and hierarchy rather than science, equality, and sustainability. Furthermore, liberal left politics has largely retreated in the contemporary era from pursuing projects rooted in conviction and making universal demands for the common good. For instance, liberals have tended to look for consensus where none can be had, such as in the Obama administration's attempts to placate right-wing extremists by further privatizing health care and gutting education and human services. At the same time, the postmodern left has tended to pursue a politics without politics through the registers of individual consumption, lifestyle choices, and a feel-good multicultural enthusiasm. In other words, a politics based on change without change.

Jacques Rancière has claimed that politics always involves *dissensus*—the act of rupturing the enclosures that fragment and deny a democratic community of equals.[9] Part of the success of neoliberal policies in education and elsewhere is that they have been rooted in convictions and claims on the universal (e.g., No Child Left Behind), although they have done so in ways that deny the very antagonisms that cut across the social order. To speak of the common is to speak of a struggle over universal claims on the future. If we consider neoliberal schooling in terms of the common, we can ask the question of how to formulate a response that recognizes the need for alternative school reform and also of how such reform might provide a basis for a new vision of a common wealth. Such a response orients a new common school movement within an unapologetic register of *dissensus*—that is, a claim on the necessity of imagining alternative ways of organizing *collective futures* beyond their reduction to neoliberal imperatives and political enclosure.

Commoning Public Alternatives

An initial proposal for a new common school movement is that it should posit both conviction and division as preconditions for an emergent community. Neoliberalism has failed as both a political and an educational project. It must therefore be opposed by an image of democracy worthy of its name. There is no alternative!

Commoning Public Control

A second proposal for a new common school movement is the project of commoning public authority and control. This involves becoming clear on how public control differs from private control. Privatization enables for-profit educational companies to skim public tax money that would otherwise be reinvested in educational services and transfer it to investor profits. These profits take concrete form in the limousines, private jets, and mansions that public tax money provides to rich investors. These profits also take symbolic form as they are used to hire public relations firms to influence parents, communities, and other investors to have faith in educational privatization and the corporation. This is a parasitical financial relationship that maximizes the potential profit for investors while cutting educational services (the expansion of primary and secondary online cyber-charter schools is the best example). This has tended to result in anti-unionism, the reduction of education to the most measurable and replicable forms, assaults on teacher autonomy, and so on. There is no evidence that the siphoning of public wealth to capitalists has improved public education or that it is required for the improvement of public education. Moreover, such redistribution shifts collective control over the processes of teaching and learning to the owner or private manager of the privatized educational approach. It captures educational labor and channels it toward profit-making for owners in the short term and future exploitable labor relations in the long term. Finally, despite claims to efficiency and innovation, neoliberal school reforms have only added to dysfunctional bureaucracy through the top-down management of decision-making and curriculum while limiting the input of educators, parents, students, and communities over school organization. Demands for an *end to privatization* and for a reinvigoration of public education should thus be combined with a path toward opening up *flexibility and democracy in the public system* in order to spur progressive innovation, enrichment, and creativity.

Commoning Public Finance

A third proposal for a new common school movement would be to rethink school finance as a common as opposed to a private matter. In a financial sense, the US public system has been privatized since its inception in that public funding has been tied to local property taxes and local real estate wealth. We might call this the *original privatization* of the public school system. Professional-class and ruling-class citizens largely purchase private educational services or more commonly move to wealthy communities—that is, they privately purchase real estate to access public schooling that is well financed and rich in resources. Working-class and poor citizens must largely make do with the lower tax receipts in urban and rural areas and underfunded schools where they can afford to live. The liberal defense of public schooling that fails to address original privatization appears to many who have been shortchanged by the historical public educational system as an unconvincing argument. This is why many working-class and poor citizens are open to the neoliberal calls for "giving the market a chance" in schooling. Of course, what is missing from this call is the recognition that historically the inequality of funding in the public system had to do with *the linkage of the public system to private wealth.* This has created what Gloria Ladson-Billings has referred to as an "educational debt" that has accrued to working-class and

African American, Latino, and Native American communities accessing the US educational system.[10]

Over the past twenty years, *neoliberal privatization* has represented an intensification of original privatization in the sense that the new privatizations take advantage of the historical de facto privatized system and the inequality it produced to further privatize and commodify schools and students who have been failed by the system. The neoliberal reforms fail to address and, in fact, exacerbate the funding inequalities of the historical public system.[11] The task of expanding a commons in public school finance involves countering both the original privatization of real estate and taxes and the more recent neoliberal privatizations. One initial solution to countering these trends is extremely simple. It would involve the United States following other industrialized nations and putting in place a federal system that ensures funding equity for all public schools and students. Despite ceaseless anxieties circulating in public discourse concerning US standing in international comparisons on standardized tests and despite the long-standing ideological presumption of upward economic mobility, the United States has the most unequally funded education system in the industrialized world and one of the worst rates of social mobility. There are a number of ways that such a national system of equalized or common funding could be achieved. It could be organized through the existing local tax system; alternatively, it could be done through the Department of Education.

Importantly, however, as Jonathan Kozol has suggested, equalizing school funding does not create the conditions for equality. The schools and students who face challenges related to poverty, home and neighborhood instability, or special needs require more investment than others. Fair funding requires progressive distribution, not equal distribution. While the quality of individual public schools and teachers does indeed matter, long-standing research indicates that educational outcomes have more to do with class disparities and social disadvantages than with differences between schools. As the research on the poor performance of charter schools relative to public schools makes clear, poor educational outcomes are intimately connected to deepening poverty, racism, joblessness, and social inequality. In other words, educational outcomes are highly dependent on the market, property, and power relations immanent to capitalist society. Thus, a fundamental aspect of commoning educational finance is a broader vision of economic justice. Such a vision would recognize that political rights are largely meaningless without a common foundation of economic rights, basic security, and common welfare. We return to these points below.

Commoning Educational Labor and Governance

A fourth proposal for a new common school movement would involve expanding common teacher and common administrator labor within a framework of common governance. As we have stated above, part of what is wrong with educational privatization is that it involves expropriating from the educational process part of the educational resources to generate profits for owners and investors. With privatization, such as in charter school expansion, teacher pay is decreased as administrator pay increases. This setup not only replicates the private-sector workforce but results in the devaluation of the teacher's labor and in deteriorating working conditions for teachers. It has also been part of an expansion of corporate culture into educational policy that seeks to downwardly distribute "accountability" while upwardly distributing rewards.

Union busting has been central to this trend of privatization through chartering. Union busting both erodes teacher control and autonomy and allows for the rapid expansion of privatization. Historically, teachers' unions have been a force for expanding teacher autonomy and equalizing control between teachers and administrators. Organizations like the New York Teachers Union and the Chicago Teachers Federation in the early twentieth century and more current instantiations like the Chicago Teachers Union under the Caucus of Rank and File Educators (CORE) have all fought against class inequality in schooling and for funding fairness and progressive curriculum. But teachers' unions have also been historically complicit in failing to challenge the status quo in schools, reproducing class hierarchy through schooling, accepting a subordinate level of control for teachers relative to administrators or accepting the teacher/administrator divide, and participating in conservative forms of pedagogy and curriculum rather than fighting for critical ones. Teachers' unions not only need to be defended in the current union-busting climate of privatization but also need to reconsider their acceptance of the labor-management arrangement throughout the history of original privatization characterizing traditional public schooling.

A crucial aim of working in common must be to establish participatory democratic governance over public educational institutions. This must involve ending the divide between teachers and administrators and between schools and communities. Teachers must be a collectively self-managed labor force at the same time that schools must be made transparent and open to the community. To put it differently, educational leadership ought to be primarily teacher leadership that is embedded within a framework of collective governance and community decision-making. The existing educational leadership establishment and district management justify themselves through the discourses of measurable accountability and disciplinary threat. To rethink accountability means the measure of educational progress should no longer be testing and standardized matrices, which are really just a performance of efficacy. Instead, *accountability in common* is realized through the extent to which schooling furthers and reflects public values and interests—that is, collective benefit, shared democratic forms of control, and improvements in communities. A new common school movement would facilitate public schooling by actually strengthening the public through the professional autonomy of teachers in a system of common values and shared responsibility and cooperation.

How do we get from here to there? One answer would be to look abroad. Finland (which happens to score best in international comparisons) provides one example. Finland has recognized that educational outcomes are inextricably tied to social conditions, and therefore, it has made commitments to ensuring all families have access to high-quality medical care, housing, and human services. In Finnish schools, teachers are imagined as professionals and public intellectuals and therefore have a high degree of pedagogical autonomy and a central role in collective school governance.

Moreover, standardized tests are rarely if ever administered to students. Thus, Finland's reforms, like those of other successful nations, are the polar opposite of what the United States has been pursuing via cuts to redistributive social services, privatization, top-down control of teachers' work, and incessant teaching to high-stakes standardized tests. A new common school movement could make central the success of models like Finland in relation to the failure of neoliberal schooling at all levels within the United States.

Another answer to commoning school governance and educational accountability can be found in the United States—in looking to recover those progressive and radical intellectual traditions associated with the original common school movement and the history of progressive and popular education. Furthermore, traditionally, the US public school system enabled the highest levels of teacher and student autonomy and community involvement in the wealthiest school districts. Therefore, relative levels of autonomy and control have tended to correspond to the future roles expected of students in the labor force in any given community. Professional-class schools prepare students to take their place as managers and leaders in the ranks of the private sector and the government. Working-class schools prepare students to take their place as low-paid, low-skill workers. Increasingly, the schools of the poor prepare students for social redundancy and economic disposability. The pedagogies that prepare professional-class students tend to encourage dialogue and debate, which are the lifeblood of collective self-governance and democratic social relations. Typically, the pedagogies that prepare working-class and low-income students of color are repressive pedagogies of control that aim for bodily discipline, are monological rather than dialogical, and promote direct instruction and testing rather than creative engagement with knowledge in common with others.

Teacher and student autonomy and community governance found in many professional-class schools need to be expanded to all schools and students, as do progressive and critical pedagogies. Together, these changes can model democratic social relations for collective endeavors outside of schools. However, modeling democracy in schools is not enough. It must be connected to broader efforts to build democratic culture and democratically redistribute human security and common welfare.

Commoning Collective Livelihoods

A fifth proposal for a new common school movement is that it should reach beyond schooling. A new common school movement must be conceived of as part of a broader process of commoning public culture, values, and economic justice. We currently inhabit a historical moment in which 25 million Americans find themselves either unemployed or underemployed, while millions more have exited the job market altogether; in which child poverty rates have hit 23 percent; in which 2.5 million Americans are captured in the nation's prisons (the majority on nonviolent drug offenses); and in which the corporate and financial elite continue to rake in record high profits, while the rest of us face stagnation, debt, and an uncertain future. Meanwhile, misguided commitments to austerity continue to hollow out commitments to education, child development, health and human services, and the labor and environmental protections necessary to secure our lives and futures.

A new common school movement must be connected to reclaiming a strong public commons that can ensure social as well as economic justice. At the core of this proposal is the need to create a new social compact that would include the right to dignified work and a guaranteed basic income; the right to a decent and affordable home; the right to medical and health care; the right to protection against economic dislocation and sickness; the right to support in old age; and the right to a free, equitable, and enriching public education. *Reviving, renewing, reimagining, and agitating* for such a commitment to public rights and protections would give progressive educators and citizens something concrete to rally around and would also work as a useful intervention in some of the most immediate and pressing issues facing working people and marginalized populations across the United States. In the short term, we could create millions of stable jobs by substantially investing in public infrastructure, in schools, and in rebuilding communities devastated by decades of neglect. This could include demands for universal early childhood education and human services for families; the modernization of school buildings; the rehiring, hiring, and investment in retention of teachers in schools and communities that will reduce class sizes and improve instruction; and the creation of new positions in schools for college and career coaches, counselors, nurses, and social workers that provide key "wraparound" services for youth. All are proven measures to enrich and enhance educational engagement and outcomes.

How do we pay for it? one might ask. Current budget realities can and must be brought into alignment with such a program of public and social investment. First, we need to close corporate tax loopholes, end corporate personhood and welfare, and raise taxes on corporations and the wealthy. It is estimated that by bringing US levels of taxation up to the Organisation for Economic Co-operation and Development (OECD) average (only a 10 percent hike), the United States would bring in additional revenue of $1.5 trillion per year and $17 or $18 trillion over ten years.[12] We need to counter the myth that taxation inhibits economic development when, in fact, such a tax increase would dramatically bolster public revenue and therefore generate the means for public investment, employment, and economic development that is locally empowered and democratic. Second, we could generate hundreds of billions in additional revenue by dismantling the military and prison-industrial complexes, ending the war on drugs (which is a public health problem, not a crime problem), raising the capital gains rates, and implementing a financial transactions tax (FST) on Wall Street. According to the Economic Policy Institute, combined with strong new financial regulation to rein in casino capitalism, an FST would raise billions of dollars per year while working to prevent the activities and excesses that led to the last financial crisis.[13]

In the long term, these measures could provide an educational and organizational basis for democratizing the economy and rethinking collective labor for common benefit. Richard Wolfe, professor of economics at the University of Massachusetts–Amherst, has suggested that we cannot limit our imagination simply to new forms of economic regulation.[14] Current global enclosures of culture, land, and labor are enacting a future of deepening inequality, human insecurity, and environmental catastrophe. Our current historical moment thus demands a broader conversation that can connect the radical imagination to fundamentally new forms of production, labor, and exchange. For Wolfe, this means looking to already existing examples of cooperatively owned and operated enterprises such as in the high-tech sector in Silicon Valley and the common management of factories in Spain and Argentina. Capitalism relies on the production of surplus value through the labor process (the differential between wages and the value produced by workers) and through the use of money as a universal means of exchange. As Marx understood well, it is a dynamic system capable of producing great wealth and technological innovation. It is also defined by periodic crisis and, without countervailing social pressures, tends toward monopoly exploitation and the erosion of land and livelihoods. As Wolfe argues, there is no practical reason that surpluses need to be accumulated by owners and executive managers, or for that matter that labor and ownership of production need to be separated at all. We must begin the difficult task of developing creative responses that push beyond the limits of capitalism and that broadly reimagine work and labor as a common as opposed to private benefit.

Education is a crucial site in this effort to invigorate radical democratic alternatives. The commons of the school includes not just the commons of the building but more importantly the common labor of teaching and learning. The most important task ahead is to reinvent the relationship between the common labor of teaching and learning and the common labor people do throughout all institutions of the society. This is an educational as well as a cultural challenge. A crucial fact about social and cultural reproduction is that capitalist reproduction can only be achieved by producing future workers with skills and know-how wrapped in capitalist ideology. To reproduce the capitalist labor force students have to learn to accept their places in the hierarchy. This is a matter of teaching values and ideology that appear as natural and uncontestable. Critical education teaches alternative values, social relations, and identifications that are contrary to those of schooling for capitalist reproduction—critical rather than dogmatic, egalitarian rather than hierarchical, collective rather than individualizing, emancipatory rather than exploitive.

Conclusion

The educational theories of John Dewey, W. E. B. Du Bois, George Counts, Paulo Freire, Henry Giroux, and others have long insisted on the centrality of public schools and classrooms as sites of democratic social transformation. Current trends in educational reform and policy, including standardization of curriculum, the common core curriculum, the "methods fetish," and high-stakes standardized testing, decontextualize knowledge and curriculum and remove them from the experiences of students and the broader social implications of what is taught and learned. These reforms run counter not just to the traditions of critical pedagogy but also to the best traditions of public schooling for progressive democracy. They represent instead redistributed control over social life and the shared substance of our being—that is, the commons.

Neoliberal reforms presume that knowledge is a deliverable commodity, something that is transmitted, rather than recognizing that knowledge is constructed through dialogic exchange, albeit always unequally. For example, the common core curriculum and its emphasis on instrumental rationalization and standardization presume that difference and different experiences are the enemy of learning. These dominant reforms deny the cultural politics of knowledge— the fact that knowledge and curriculum represent contested material interests and ideological positions. Such reforms deny the subjective interests and positions of those making claims to truth and those interpreting the claims of others. The dominant reforms also deny objective social conditions and represent an assault on individual judgment, denial of the necessary interpretation of experience, and the reality that individual and social assumptions undergird practices. To put it differently, the dominant reforms actively produce social and political illiteracy in teachers and students. Although this is a convenient form of production in terms of social control by elites, it does not bode well for a society theoretically committed to the democratic values of equality, freedom, and justice.

Critical pedagogy's value for experience rejects the assumption that experience "speaks for itself" or is transparently true. Instead, critical pedagogy insists that experience always needs to be interpreted—that is, theorized in terms of broader objective realities and social forces. Dominant educational reforms presume that experience is largely transparent and that knowledge is always neutral and does not require interpretation. For example, the new teacher accreditation standards of the single accrediting body, the Council for the Accreditation of Educator Preparation (CAEP), place clinical practice at the center and forefront of teacher preparation, discarding the crucial step of preparing teacher candidates with the theoretical tools to interpret what they witness in classrooms. The teacher candidate who witnesses the urban classroom with its shocking levels of poverty and racial segregation needs the theoretical tools to make sense of, for example, the origins and reproduction of concentrated poverty and racism; disinvestment in schools, public services, and communities; generalized social fragmentation in an age of austerity and social abandonment; and the way that all of these processes order students' experiences in direct and subtle ways. Teachers must be able to link the experiences of students to the social conditions that produce and inform those experiences globally. And teachers must be able to link the social locations and conditions of students to explorations within the curriculum. Such limitations in interpretive tools result in the majority of teacher candidates failing to comprehend such immediate and practical matters as student motivation or lack of it and the related dropout crisis. Similarly, the denial of critical and interpretive tools for teacher candidates allows no purchase on the ways that systemic and symbolic violence play out powerfully in classrooms, such as when students equate book learning with the history and culture of Eurocentrism and white supremacy.

A new common school movement must establish fundamentally new ways of learning and thinking in relation to our global commonality and our shared fate. This necessarily means rethinking curriculum, teaching, and learning in ways that recover the radical impulse of the progressive and critical tradition and that push beyond this tradition as well. We imagine this global horizon as pedagogy in common. In what follows, we elaborate on how a new common school movement must make *pedagogy in common* central to the reconstruction of schooling.

◆

CHAPTER **6**

Toward a Pedagogy in Common

As we have pointed out, while neoliberalism and the processes of globalization that it shapes are rightly understood as a political-economic strategy for recuperating a ruling-class interest and vision, they also importantly precipitate a condition of tremendous instability and uncertainty at the level of the lifeworld—that is, the frameworks of meaning within which we live our everyday lives. After all, the collapse of experience and identity into the bottom-line logic of quantitative indices and benchmarks that neoliberalism undertakes in the sphere of education and elsewhere is in the final analysis a process of violence and erasure rather than simply a reframing. Quite simply, the objective and subjective worlds that we inhabit cannot, in truth, be represented by such metrics—and so are fundamentally distorted, or disappear, when they must be accounted for in this way. For this reason, we should recognize that the problem that neoliberalism poses for education and society is not just political (in a narrow sense) but deeply pedagogical as well. That is, the kind of colonization of experience that neoliberalism undertakes and, on the other hand, the horizon of the common that a democratic education should seek to explore are two sides of a struggle over basic senses and textures of knowing, communicating, and learning that are necessarily implicated in pedagogy. Teaching is a fundamental moment in the becoming of selves, understandings, and relationships. On the one hand, this means that it is touched in a special

67

way by a model of social life that would flatten these terrains into dimensionless occasions of measurement and manipulation. On the other hand, it suggests that the moment of teaching is a crucial one for the emerging common, since in announcing the very possibilities of self and community, teaching in a sense invents the common itself.

We have so far described the broad crisis currently confronting education as well as the critical choices we face in the present with regard to how we understand and struggle for democratic educational transformation. In this chapter, we bring these concerns to the terrain of teaching itself. The project of *pedagogy in common* has to respond not just to the limitations that are insisted on by reductionist and scripted curriculum and assessment but also to the experience of imposition and insecurity that the neoliberal educational program institutes. Far from settling teaching and learning into a comfortable and reassuring routine, the aggressive reconstruction of schooling by the logic of efficiency and the paradigm of the market has the effect of introducing radical uncertainty and anxiety into education, as the literal fates of students, teachers, and schools hang in the balance of official test score reports and as the very content and meaning of education are wrested from the participants, who are forced to await the shifting dictates of distant administrators to discover what it now means to teach, learn, and know.

A new common school movement must be able to envision new forms of pedagogy and curriculum, both in school settings and in the context of struggles for democracy, at the same time that it critiques the larger landscape of educational politics and policy. We first consider here how teaching and learning are touched by neoliberalism's assault on and reordering of subjectivity and sociality. We then propose, in response, several important principles for building critical, democratic, and enlivening forms of pedagogy and curriculum in the present; we call these principles, taken together, *pedagogy in common.* As we describe, these principles suggest concrete interventions in the classroom context as well as crucial modes of engagement in cultural and political work. We should point out that a central premise of our argument is that the common, and the pedagogy in common that works toward it, are always *under construction.* For this reason, we do not aim to provide any simple blueprints, but rather to begin a process of analysis and imagination that we hope will be taken up by others who share our commitment to a democratic education against and beyond neoliberalism.

The Crisis of Teaching and Curriculum

Neoliberal programs for teaching and curriculum have to be seen not only as offensives to reorient the ideological space of education in the interest of a market-driven and corporatist culture but also as a defensive effort to elaborate fluid control over a crucial moment and site of the common, as the space of the classroom is wrenched free from traditional modes of epistemological authority by the radical challenges to tradition introduced by globalization and democratic movements. The compulsive rituals of measurement and scholasticism—which extend far beyond test preparation itself into the texture of regular instruction, as schools are gripped by a generalized performance anxiety—can be seen as efforts to produce a provisional order for a space that is at risk of a fundamental disorientation. The proliferation of pedagogical ranking systems for "achievement" and "success" (at the micro as much as at the macro level) enforces individualism and competitiveness, but also desperately seeks to fill the space of school with *some* goal and ethos—as the old rationales are undone or fade away.

The crisis that confronts education at the classroom level, in terms of the kind of community it produces among students and teachers and the everyday interactions that structure the meanings of teaching and learning, has two important aspects. At the *epistemological-curricular* level, knowledge is fragmented by the obsession with measurement and objectives, and the provincialism of traditional curriculum is challenged in the context of globalization. At the *practical-pedagogical* level, the stakes of educational relationships are increased as communication becomes a crucial medium of work in post-Fordism, and consequently, as the kinds of dialogue that teaching produces directly intervene in one way or another in the process of social production. While elites seek to recover familiar forms of authority or to invent new ones more suited to contemporary conditions, democratic efforts oriented toward a pedagogy in common seek to create spaces for new meanings and forms of community oriented toward collective solidarity. While the form that globalization has taken has been organized by institutions and firms centered in the global North, it has also posed a challenge to the nation as the framework for sovereignty as well as for individual and collective identity. Fulfilling capitalism's tendency (famously noted by Marx and Engels) to overrun traditional orders of authority, globalization in the present contains a challenge to the provincialism even of hegemonic nation-based cultural and political formations. (This is the kernel of truth hidden at the bottom of paranoid right-wing fantasies of a global conspiracy to annex the United States and its "way of life.") At the same time, movements and intellectuals in the global South have challenged the North's insistence on reserving for itself, in Said's terms, "an invisible point of super-objective perspective,"[1] while rejecting a process of globalization organized in the interest of the transnational capitalist class (which is itself dominated by capitalists in North America and Europe). Extending the anti-colonial liberation movements of the post–World War II period into the terrain of knowledge and culture and sharpening the postcolonial critique of the Eurocentric framework of Western culture, *decolonial* theorists have proposed a project of delinking from the dominative knowledge formations that have supported empire and refused non-European epistemologies.[2] The epistemological foundations of the West, and Western education, are in this way fundamentally interrogated.

In addition, as Paolo Virno describes, the destabilization we experience in late capitalism exposes us not just to familiar fears about job security but also to a more basic anguish connected to an underlying condition of existential homelessness, as we are torn from the refuges of particular habits and identities—as these are dissolved in post-Fordism—and thrown into the unmoored universality of the multitude.[3] In this way, neoliberal globalization is partly responsible for the cultural disorientation that it then seeks to contain through disciplinary and ideological strategies. The insecurity of this transition contains resistant possibilities, since in being forced from idiosyncratic habits and identities, we are at the same time forced into the terrain of "common places"—the basic and shared potentials of thought and language—that are proper to us as human beings and on the basis of which new collective projects and praxis are possible. In this regard, the neoliberal pedagogical formations of the current period should be understood in part as efforts to colonize the opening that globalization's destabilizations introduce, and to co-opt the increasingly coordinated networks of knowledge and information that really belong to all of us.

Anti-democratic efforts to contain this crisis in curriculum and teaching—or more broadly in knowledge (epistemology) and practice (praxis)—head in one of two directions. In the first place, the contemporary period has seen a significant rise in right-wing reaction both in the political landscape generally and in the educational sphere in particular. However, while the Tea Party movement has often cloaked its revanchist impulses in the apparently colorless politics of fiscal conservatism (in fact, a white-knuckled and vengeful drive for extreme austerity), in education the right has unabashedly called for a rolling back of progressive and multicultural inroads in curriculum and for a return to a "traditional" cultural consensus. In the most celebrated recent case, Texas revised its social studies standards to celebrate American capitalism, de-emphasize historical forms of inequity and oppression (racism in particular), marginalize the historical contributions of people of color, and polish the image of the Republican Party. As Heilig, Brown, and Brown show, while including progressive figures and movements in optional content lists, the revised standards consolidate a white and conservative vision of US history and society within the mandatory curriculum tied to high-stakes tests.[4] Although at one level this is a continuation of the culture wars of the 1990s, reactionary curricular initiatives in the present should also be seen as defensive efforts to respond to the increasing instability of the cultural and epistemological consensus.

The second direction in the effort to contain this crisis is the properly neoliberal one. Expressing on the terrain of curriculum late capitalism's broader reengineering of the political and social contract, *procedurally oriented* approaches to teaching—and indeed the proliferation of scripted and packaged curricula across grade levels—work to tame cognition toward the form of the test and away from uncharted and autonomous investigations. In this process, the ideological work that education does is less evident in the content and dispositions that it seeks to embed in the popular common sense and more in the form itself of the procedural and bureaucratic complex that it produces through processes of instruction and assessment. Scripted curricula are typically characterized by a formidable array of "alignment" and "focus" matrices—tied to official state standards—that organize the process of learning in terms of a complex ritual. While this procedure-driven teaching can collaborate with a reactionary cultural politics, there is also a tension between neoliberal accountability initiatives and rightist interventions, since the former have a relativizing effect on knowledge that the latter seek to resist.

Under the tyranny of this new proceduralism, schooling comes to be colonized by the spreading "prison time" of late capitalism.[5] Ostensibly set free into the wilderness of *choice* (to apply oneself or not, to succeed or to fail), students are, in fact, ever more intimately invaded by neoliberalism as biopolitical regime, their bodies and minds continuously tethered to the form of the objective and the test. For students who resist, schooling can become a process of endless remediation, but even "successful" students now encounter learning as a kind of boundless detention—within the persistent process of auditing that teaching has become. The racial economy of capitalism sets the scale here, as students of color are much more likely to face serious discipline and punishment, and much more likely to be excluded altogether—as push-outs—from school.[6]

Against these strategies of disposal and containment, a radically democratic path out of the current crisis should seek not to evade it but rather to *work through it* collaboratively toward a different kind of knowing and doing. Challenging the deep impulse of the West to deny the value of other perspectives and understandings, a pedagogy in common should welcome the crisis of dominative epistemologies and should work toward the coexistence of different standpoints in education—as well as diverse curricular projects based on them—while giving a strategic priority to perspectives marginalized by imperialism and Eurocentrism.[7] Furthermore, within the classroom, an approach to teaching based on the common should challenge both the old forms of pedagogical hierarchy that have supplied the teacher's authority and the new forms that are crystallized by the control of the accountability apparatus. It is worth pointing out that one crucial aspect of contemporary global student movements against the neoliberalization of education (from Santiago to Montreal) is the effort to reclaim for students not only the right to learn but also *the authority to know*—as young people have enacted a radically authoritative knowledge of themselves and the institutions that capture them—against the official neoliberal "reality" of despair and impossibility.

Starting Points for Pedagogy: Three Figures

Teaching in the present faces the difficult set of circumstances described above. This "limit-situation," as Freire described the existential-historical challenges that confront those engaged in liberatory praxis,[8] has as one of its special features the displacement of the confrontation itself, as ideological contests in the present are obscured by the very procedures of schooling. Power works now less to interpellate students as proper citizen-subjects through the operation of the hidden curriculum, and more to fracture and control them as partial subject-effects of education as measurement and auditing. To put it another way, as the mode of production of society is increasingly distributed and networked, the struggle is less over the moral framing of the individual's relationship to work and the state than over the purposes and possibilities of shared networks of knowledge and information. Against the offensive and defensive measures of neoliberal globalization, a democratic form of education has to intervene not to restore the limited vision of inquiry in liberal and progressive models but rather to link teaching and learning to alternative and forward-looking visions of praxis that refuse the containment of the social imagination.

This vision of liberatory education, which we call *pedagogy in common*, is oriented within the intellectual tradition of critical pedagogy while simultaneously seeking to deepen and extend this tradition through engagements with the commons. To this end, a pedagogy in common foregrounds the commons as a site of both contestation and social production. In other words, alongside the crucial work of uncovering possibilities of agency and community through the *negative* (the critical analysis and deconstruction of the hegemonic), we also need to challenge the limits of the dominant in the process of *producing* different and emancipatory modes of knowing and being together. This is not to de-emphasize the importance of informed criticism and the role of struggle; on the contrary, realizing truly democratic forms of society and education means a difficult fight against the forces organized against them. What we want to emphasize here is the need to consider how education can become a powerful force for the social production of alternative forms of community and enactment of the global commons. In this way, rather than radical hope confronting a deadening reality, an emergent emancipatory reality (the collective production of the common) *confronts power's own desperate hope*: to cling to the impossible limits of the given.

Before it is a set of strategies or even a philosophy, pedagogy is a way of being with other people. Teaching is primarily a set of relationships and modes of engagement. It is linked to other social occasions and possibilities, and in this way, it counts as a crucial political moment, since the relationships it creates can mimic broader relations of domination or begin to realize liberatory alternatives. In addition, it has a special charge: in the responsibility it has to organize learning, pedagogy mediates the basic link in society between ways of being and ways of knowing. In the context of education, not only does knowledge become political but also relationships become epistemological. The next chapter will come at this situation from the vantage point of knowledge and curriculum; in this chapter, we consider it in terms of modes of engagement (praxis) and pedagogy and suggest several ways of approaching the task of building the common in education. We believe that these forms of engagement, which we present as basic modes or figures, are linked to broader political struggles and forms of democratic citizenship; at the same time, they can usefully frame concrete interventions at the classroom level.

1. Rupture

This first mode of pedagogy and praxis involves a challenge to the machinery that governs contemporary schooling. In the context of an encompassing control that seeps as much into the performances of teaching as into the everyday experience of students, this challenge has first of all to take the form of a break and refusal, rather than a simple critique. Neoliberal accountability regimes recompose the subjectivities of educators within a managerial and entrepreneurial frame while practically transforming the process of teaching into a ritual of skills-oriented training and assessment.[9] Contemporary scripted curriculum, test preparation, and classroom management regimes demand that teachers do more than endorse a set of values; rather, they must act as the effective instrument of schooling as procedure. In this way, neoliberal education aims to reconstruct not only beliefs but even subjectivity itself—for both teachers and students. It is difficult in the first instance for educators to argue with this process, since they come to literally embody it in their performances in the classroom.

One can understand this shift in the mode of power in schools in terms of the idea that capitalism in the present is characterized by a logic of *command* rather than simply incorporation;[10] increasingly, schooling aims as much to exclude and decompose students as it does to assimilate them. The push-out problem, in which "low-performing" students are passively encouraged to quit for the sake of raising test scores, the school-to-prison pipeline, and the racist coding of students of color as irremediable and disposable convert education from a process of enforcing dominant forms of "common sense" into what Noah De Lissovoy has called a process of *violation*.[11] In this context, the first task of the teacher is to *refuse to act as the agent of injury*. The challenge is that this injury is built into the structure of the normal expectations and habits that make up what teaching and learning have become. Rupture, in this case, means a difficult turn away from given habits and procedures.

In the era of accountability, this problem is often expressed in the ethical dilemma posed by standardized testing regimes. Should teachers work around the edges and make the best of the space that is left to them outside of testing and test preparation, or should they undertake a more radical break? In our view, ultimately teachers will need to find a way to refuse to participate in the scripting of pedagogy as preparation for assessment. Effective refusal of this regime will need to be organized and collective, to give individuals the moral and material support necessary to resist. Although this form of rupture/refusal is sometimes difficult for educators to contemplate, when undertaken simultaneously with the forms of engagement we describe below, it can become easier to imagine—since it then becomes part of a positive vision and process.

2. Project

In the first instance, the emphasis on projects in teaching is a familiar progressive educational idea. Dewey insisted that educators go beyond the simple transmission of detached and decided content, and instead undertake a teaching that is purpose-oriented, collaborative, and related to social context. Various instructional approaches in the present, including "project-based learning," emphasize the importance of connecting instruction to authentic purposes and engaging students in an extended collaborative process in which they learn academic content in the course of working together rather than in an artificial and decontextualized manner. From this perspective, in working together toward the accomplishment of something meaningful to them, students can be more powerfully engaged in learning. In the current educational context, even these familiar recommendations acquire a radical tinge.

However, progressive project-oriented approaches generally fail to explore the underlying political assumptions that set the terms for teaching; they also suffer from a lack of imagination in their sense of the collective subject that takes shape in an educational project. Even Dewey takes democratic society as a more or less given referent for teaching. By contrast, as those in the tradition of critical pedagogy like Paulo Freire, Henry Giroux, and others have long insisted, thinking *pedagogy as project* involves the production of new teaching and learning subjects—and new subjects of democracy.[12] That is to say, the notion of project is as much about the production of subjectivity as it is about the realization of objective aims. In a broader context, Hardt and Negri argue for a collective revolutionary subject that in *making itself* precipitates the emancipatory possibilities of the common.[13] Similarly, we should reframe our sense of the *projective* in pedagogy—highlighting this category as a radical opening up of the possibilities of both politics and subjectivity toward the transformation of our economic and institutional frameworks by making them accountable to the commons.

From this perspective, educational projects should include efforts that engage students in study of and intervention in their communities and public life. But in addition, refusing the limits of the given, in a pedagogy in common, teaching and learning construct new communities on their own terms. This does not mean these communities are not crucially affected by their surroundings; it only means that in deciding their basic forms and purposes they are not limited to a reactive orientation. Perhaps the crucial site for this form of engagement in the current conjuncture has been Tahrir Square. The Egyptian Revolution was mobilized by the demand that Mubarak step down, but more importantly, it lived and grew through the new community that was built in Tahrir. Its vitality was in its making of a different kind of being together, and in the process it produced both a new social subject (a new "Egypt") and a new common space of collaboration, action, and communication.

Similarly, students and educators have recently experimented with various forms of autonomous university set free from the neoliberal economy and epistemology that increasingly govern higher education.[14] These have grown from mass protests against what might be called the "ownership university"; however, student movements in the present *look beyond* this university at the same time that they resist it. In the context of K–12 schooling, the recent struggle over the ethnic studies program in the Tucson, Arizona, schools illustrates the reaction provoked by community-based and projective pedagogy. In an active rather than a reactive stance, the Raza Studies program in Tucson aimed first of all to *create* an affirming, critical, and rigorous educational space for Chicana/o students. Nevertheless, its delinking from dominant frameworks was portrayed by white officials as an attack.[15] *Imagination, affirmation, project*: these pedagogical modalities are especially threatening to power, since they refuse to be constrained even by the frame of subversion and critique (although subversion and critique are crucial moments within them).

3. Conversation

The notion of *conversation*, understood in a militantly democratic frame, can be useful in framing a common pedagogy in
the present. The tradition of critical pedagogy has rightfully
been suspicious of this term, concerned that in contrast to
the depth implied in *dialogue*, the model of conversation
may suggest a superficial exchange of opinions. It is true
that the conversations that proliferate in mainstream media
and in official political debates usually amount to little more
than sterile chatter. But conversation can be understood
differently: *as a collaborative investigation of reality, and
as a mobilization of collective imagination against power.* In
this sense, conversation can be thought of as a polycentric
dialogue that seeks to awaken the outrage and creativity of a
community. This sense of conversation multiplies the force of
dialogue as well as democratizing it, since it pushes beyond
the dyadic logic of the latter toward a praxis generated from
a multiplicity of participants.

There is useful pedagogical precedent for this idea in the
notion of a *community of learners*, as this emerges from the
cultural-historical tradition in education.[16] This understanding decenters pedagogical authority from individual teachers
to a cultural community as a whole and investigates the
processes of apprenticeship that bring learners and teachers
together in a shared network of culture and cognition. Within
the radical frame of the common school movement that we
propose, however, the political indeterminacy of this model
needs to be challenged, as does the notion of expertise on
which it depends. Unhinged from the authority of tradition,
what emancipatory purposes might such learning communities invent? Likewise, set free from the sedimented expertise
of teachers or elders, what power might students find for
themselves? In the context of neoliberal schooling, progressive, sociocultural, and critical educational approaches
should take seriously the overdetermination of the vested
authority of the teacher by procedure and punishment, even
when we do our best to humanize this authority by making
it responsive to the commons. Against authority as procedure and punishment, a democratic form of pedagogical
authority needs to be based in what we described above as
accountability in common that recognizes teacher autonomy

and authority as rooted in a shared commitment to common learning for collective benefit. Such a commitment has the potential to enact and make concrete what Jacques Rancière has referred to as a "community of equals" beyond neoliberal fragmentation.[17]

The model of conversation also points to the importance, in the era of knowledge capitalism, of the sphere of communication. Challenging the theory/practice binary, this model proposes a praxis in which these poles partly overlap. In the present, interventions on the terrain of cultural politics can set the parameters for material struggles, but the latter can crucially affect the framing of political narratives. For instance, the 2012 strike by Chicago teachers succeeded in at least stalling the corporatist attack on working conditions for educators in that city. At the same time, it was a crucial intervention on the terrain of political discourse and discussions of the labor movement, as the union demonstrated its strength, its concern for students, and its commitment to public schools. Similarly, the national movement that has arisen in opposition to the racist demonization of Latina/o immigrants by the state and civil society has not so much sought to "change the conversation" as to *bring a different conversation* into the public sphere—a human conversation, the conversation of the Dreamers, a conversation for respect and dignity for all.

◇

Chapter 7

Globalization, the Common, and Curriculum

As we have argued, "the common" is a name both for an actually emergent experience of interconnectedness and for a utopian political project. We are reconstructed by globality at the same time as we participate in inventing it. Whether these processes are truly simultaneous depends on the degree to which globalization is available to democratic interventions. If we are committed to the realization of a democratic global common, then the process and mode of our engagement are crucial problems. To grapple with these problems, we have to consider them *educationally*. After all, the production of an unprecedented social condition is essentially a process of learning and teaching. In the field of education proper, this rethinking of the pedagogy of democracy is especially urgent.

Rethinking Curriculum in Global Context

Understanding the itinerary of the common that we have described—from the historical moment of enclosure to the utopian horizon of the global—has important implications for the curriculum in particular, especially where this means not simply the manifest content of education but also the ideological and epistemological foundations of this content. In the first place, being sensitive to the emergence of the condition of transnationalism and of a "transnational imaginary"

in curriculum,[1] implies an unraveling of the national identifications that anchor student and teacher subjectivities and
that are painstakingly constructed through the experience of
schooling itself—in the US case, in the rituals of the Pledge
of Allegiance, the celebrations of the "founding fathers," and
the often perfunctory gestures of multicultural inclusion.
This involves the ideological work of challenging our basic
interpellation as national subjects. This is a traumatic process, to the extent that the very matrix of intelligibility that
founds our own coherence to ourselves begins to fray. In this
context, teachers and learners in a democratic pedagogy in
the global context—or pedagogy in common—are called on
to join in the production of an unprecedented form of global
citizenship. Rather than a simple concern for the fates of
others elsewhere, this means a political project of alliance
and an intellectual project of discovering the purposes that
determine our shared, and different, situations.

Even progressive approaches that seek to build more
genuine ethical spaces are often captured by a provincialism
that does not recognize that the privileges of the pluralism of
the global North depend on the refusal of a responsibility to
the "periphery." Valuing diverse experiences and challenging
processes of social exclusion have not usually been thought
of as projects to be undertaken collectively at the global
level; multicultural education, for instance, has only recently
begun to consider this context.[2] However, attending carefully
to globalization, and to the historical passages of colonialism and imperialism that have contributed to constructing
it, necessarily transforms our understanding of racism and
marginalization. Progressive efforts to include minority
populations often ignore the inscription of majority-minority
relations in histories of conquest as well as in contemporary
neocolonial economic and political projects globally. Additionally, these approaches often neglect the conceptual and
political unraveling of the authority and autonomy of the
"center" that is implied by a global perspective. In the United
States, it is often overlooked that the reproduction of life and
culture in the North is absolutely dependent, on the ground
floor, on global flows of cheap labor from the South, and at the
heights, on global flows of finance capital from the East. The
allegiance to US exceptionalism that is mandatory in public
discourse, and in education as well, is an expression of the

defensiveness that characterizes the attitude of a declining global hegemon. However, within a pedagogy in common, it is a discourse we should crucially contest.

As we have argued, authentic solidarity with others elsewhere means an understanding of the logic of capitalist accumulation, especially in its neoliberal manifestation. There are important implications here for the selection of explicit content. The history of the "market," so touted in the popular media, can be retold from the standpoint of the victims of enclosure (from the feudal period in Europe to the contemporary dispossessions wrought by neoliberalism), and with attention to the new global society that is produced by the flows of capital, information, and people—and to its economic, technological, and communicative potential. A pedagogy in common calls for a curriculum of trade and economics that would look beyond conventional accounts of development to critical analyses of the social and environmental ravages caused by the ubiquitous processes of marginalization and privatization, as well as discussing the spaces created by movements of popular protest and alternative practices. For instance, experiments against corporate intellectual property (alternative forms of copyright, legal challenges to patents by transnational corporations of indigenous knowledge, open-source programming, etc.) ought to be made available to young people as alternative visions of production and ownership anchored in and dependent upon the collective, increasingly on a transnational scale.

However, the most powerful implications for critical education of emerging senses of global democracy are the potential transformations in educational relationships that they suggest. In moments of transition, education becomes a staging ground, or experimental space, for larger democratic projects. Contemporary anti-systemic movements are characterized by a collaborative and networked form of organization that does not depend, to the same degree, on the personalities of leaders as have earlier movements. There are important lessons to be drawn from these movements. For instance, we need to affirm the autonomy of teachers; at the same time, curriculum and instruction need to undertake a reconstruction of the authority of the teacher beyond their instrumental reduction to procedure and transmission. Moreover, and crucially, we need to recognize the democratic agency and autonomy of students themselves. We can see this independent agency of students in the many contemporary student-led walkouts, protests, and activist organizations that link school reform to issues of immigration, militarization, and economic opportunity. Only this kind of loosening of the epistemological and political limits of teaching can liberate the collaborative imagination that will be necessary to confront a rapidly changing global society and to participate in building its future. Beyond familiar efforts to build on prior knowledge, this principle suggests a basic revaluation in which the minds of students are no longer expected to be folded into the superior intelligence of the curriculum. Instead, student and teacher thinking each become independent and indispensable starting points for intellectual and practical interventions in common.

Just as it means a shift in the organization of educational authority, the urgency of building a form of democracy adequate to the global moment also corresponds to a shift in the purposes of education. In contrast to the retrospective orientation of Dewey's *reconstructionism*, which sought to reorder and improve existing knowledge and social relationships,[3] the curricular approach we describe here could be understood as a radical departure from the given—a forward-looking and audacious *constructionism* that is motivated by the emergency of responding to the crises of neoliberal globalization. The focus of curriculum within such a philosophy is less to initiate students into the wisdom and practices of the culture and more to provoke them to the discovery of the knowledge and society of the future. The justification for this break with familiar and progressive senses of educational purpose is the special character of the crises that confront us in the present. The new forms of anomie that emerge with the destruction of national identifications, and the desperation of populations abandoned to their fates by the global market and by the breakdown of the communicative rationality of politics, cannot be parsed by the social science that is currently available to students.[4] (Consider, for example, the failure of the "leading democratic societies" to respond creatively to the challenges of genocide, climate change, or economic collapse; the discourses that produce these failures are codified in the curricula of social studies and citizenship classrooms.) In methodological terms, this means challenging Dewey's basic principle of the *continuity* of the curriculum (its progressive building on and rearticulation of accomplished understandings).[5] In the present, we require a radically *discontinuous* learning, one that can propose unprecedented modes of thought and practice. This form of education does not just respect but essentially depends on the intelligence of students and generates a form of knowledge that refuses the familiar determinations.

The proposals described above will have to confront the current articulation of the basic meanings of education within the hegemonic logic of neoliberalism—the dramatic attenuation of the space for critical teaching through the imposition of positivistic benchmarking of achievement, scripted and corporate-sponsored curricula, and narrow senses of literacy. However, the point is not to envision a top-down reorganization of curriculum, but rather to urge teachers in their own contexts to be sensitive to social and political shifts already taking place on the ground and among students and to be aware of the possibilities of a pedagogy built on the basis of these organic processes.

In this regard, several important practical implications of this approach are outlined here. First, teachers can create space in their classrooms for the investigation of emerging forms of alternative and youth cultures and movements, as they are lived in and out of school, and in particular as they knit together disparate and transnational contexts. Scholars have described the emancipatory potential of hip-hop, which is already a thoroughly global idiom, often allied with forms of political resistance internationally.[6] Less reported on are the emerging diasporas of *rock en español, norteño,* and other Latin American popular musical genres that contribute to a transnational identification for youth from immigrant families. These popular cultural forms are linked to concrete struggles by young people against the creeping criminalization of youth by law enforcement and anti-immigrant initiatives while revealing the ongoing recoding and transnationalization of working-class culture. Likewise, as youth in the United States begin to participate in efforts to reclaim public space for a new urban cultural and ecological commons, as for example in the inner-city community gardens of the Detroit Agriculture Network,[7] they can be helped to investigate the connections between these efforts and international ones—such as worker occupations of shuttered factories in Argentina and peasant movements against corporate development projects in India—to defend collective space and resources from appropriation and privatization. In making the classroom hospitable to discussion of these movements and supporting students' own initiatives as activists and cultural workers engaged in critical praxis, teachers can expand the terrain for radical democratic work without appropriating from the students the sole authority to direct it.

In addition, in response to the official and reductionistic forms of teaching and learning noted above, the senses of the global common that we have described suggest site-specific investigations of local *educational* conditions in relationship to larger contexts. For instance, to explore the way that administrative rationality and privatization efforts come together in neoliberal social policy globally, teachers can foreground (as crucial examples of this policy) the pervasive testing regimes that they confront along with their students. Rather than simply trying to elude these constraints, teachers and students might systematically investigate their global origins, meanings, and effects. In fact, while there is a long history of critical accounts of standardized assessments, we have seen the emergence more recently of teacher-student coalitions specifically organized against them. These organizations have begun to draw connections between the racial and class inequalities that accountability regimes reinforce and the global strategies of capital. Not only do such efforts make crucial analytic links but they experiment with new forms of authority and solidarity that decenter the traditional teacher-leader. For example, in the Brazilian Citizen School, there is a collective process of decision-making (extending even to curricula and budgets) explicitly oriented against the managerialism of capital's social and educational "best practices."[8]

Finally, in support of all of these efforts, critically oriented teacher-preparation programs should dramatically expand opportunities for future educators to consider the underlying issues at stake: the sense and direction of neoliberalism and globalization, the articulation between education and social movements, and the meaning of democracy itself. This would mean, among other things, a rigorous exposure to contemporary social and political theory. While these recommendations, by themselves, will not defeat the overwhelming force of anti-democratic discourses and practices in schools, together they can help to facilitate the entry into education of broader movements for global democracy.

Education and the Social Production of the Commons

Our discussions of the meanings of the democratic common above are premised on the idea that its production involves a basic challenge to the order of actually existing society. Although we have discussed some of the most important implications of an understanding of the common for the practices of educators, it is crucial to see that education is not merely a dependent variable in this relation. In fact, education as much determines the sense and form of the common as it is a simple field of practical application of the common as philosophical and political concept.

There are three ways in which education is itself partly *constitutive* of the shared social condition and experience that is the common: (1) education is one of the most essential moments of collectivity or being together, in any society, and therefore one of the most crucial terrains for ongoing experimentation with the meanings of social relationships and collaboration; (2) in its extension across society and its engagement with young people, education is perhaps the most important tool for reorganizing social and cultural life and for consolidating new and more democratic processes; (3) the specific kind of encounter and communication between subjects that takes place in education—in which basic meanings and identifications are offered, taken up, and renegotiated—imprints itself on the emerging common as part of its essence. Politics is always essentially a teaching and a learning, rather than a static and objective system of ideas. In other words, if we want to build a new and more democratic and just global society, the point is not to produce a blueprint of that society that we then execute or implement but rather to begin a collective and organic process of *education*—a process in which the social body slowly teaches itself a new way of being.

In explaining how a new society emerges from within the interstices of contemporary capitalism, De Angelis describes a provisional shift in "value practices" that is felt in the fleeting moments of struggle and social movement: "Experiencing commons in which we have to take responsibility for our daily actions and reproduction, safety, goals and aspirations ... means articulating social co-production according to different values, it means experimenting and trying out different value practices, it means making an *outside* dimension to the value practices of capital *visible*."[9] In other words, struggles against privatization, war, and marginalization are not simply negative moments of protest but positive moments in which new temporalities, values, and practices tentatively begin to suggest a different social world. These are inherently pedagogical projects, since what has not been permitted before we have to collectively teach ourselves—which is no doubt why education is such a priority in the Zapatista indigenous autonomous zones of Chiapas, for example, and in general why the alternative globalization movements so strongly emphasize training for participants in new forms of decision-making and collective action. But beyond these disparate moments, it is important to see that education will be crucial in organizing and consolidating any new global democratic sociality—not because education should enforce its order on all, after the manner of the schooling we are familiar with, but rather because education can provide the space for teachers and students to experiment with and refine the original and unanticipated forms of a democratic community that is already inherently an invention.

To this end, it is important to radicalize two central principles in the progressive understanding of the relation between democracy and education. First, in this tradition there is a basic relationship between education and society not just to the extent that democratic education teaches *about* democracy but also insofar as this education begins to inculcate the rich and complex relationships, and "conjoint communicated experience,"[10] that characterize democratic societies. Democracy is not simply a form of government but a form of life, and to the extent that its possibilities are enlarged both by the horizon of globality itself and by movements of opposition to neoliberalism, democratic education must be responsive to these developments. That is, education should begin to explore the new networks of relationships, horizontal forms of association, and bottom-up forms of decision-making that are respectively proposed by the Internet, transnational progressive alliances, and indigenous movements at the same time that it must engage in projects to redefine our local and global institutional structures on the basis of redistributive control over common wealth for collective benefit.

Second, progressive and critical pedagogies emphasize the *experimental* character of education, on the basis of which the teacher is responsible for creating the parameters within which the intelligence of students can freely explore the social world. But our sense of experimentation today should be broader, extending to the collective investigation and practice, by teachers and students together, of *new* democratic values, norms, and practices—ones that do not reside at the core of existing society as its ideal, but rather press against it from the outside, as premonitions of a different order of collective life. Here, too, it is important to emphasize the indeterminate meaning of "democracy," an idea that has been enrolled into oppressive as well as liberatory systems and movements. Identifying this term with a fundamentally imaginative social project, as we do here, means constructing at the same time a new discursive field for "democracy" itself, as a practice of emancipation whose limits cannot be set ahead of time by any instrumentalism.

In this experimentation, pedagogy works on the sense and organization of its own relationships and, at the same time, presages and precipitates the basic meanings of a new democratic society. What we have called above *pedagogy in common* experiments with the basic kind of offering that education is, reframing this offering not as the transmission of a reified knowledge, nor simply as the invitation to a critical habit of mind, but rather as the proposal of a moment of collective invention. In this process, the teacher's job is not to ensure the coherence of a controlled experiment but to provoke an investigation whose outcome cannot be anticipated. Just as the context of the global undoes the boundaries of our senses of community and culture, in the same way pedagogy in common undoes the boundaries of our senses of teaching and learning. The teaching situation, in this context, is more than a laboratory for the construction of new (or reconstructed) knowledge; it becomes a laboratory for the construction of new modes of relationship and collective activity, and thus of social life itself. This project depends on a generosity that recognizes that the possibilities that the teacher makes available to students must be fundamentally reorganized by them. This is a kind of teaching that not only recognizes the validity of students' agency and knowledge but even depends on them, not as settled powers but as open-ended processes and potentialities. The significance of this educational conception is not just methodological but also political. Education brings together processes of meaning-making and modes of articulation of authority in a way that no other situation does; how it chooses to combine these sets the limits for democracy and community more broadly.

Our discussion points to the centrality of education to larger projects of democracy and community building. A movement that seeks to realize the senses of the common that we have described will have to recognize the importance of a pedagogical engagement. This is necessary first of all because education is perhaps the most important space for construction and consolidation of new forms of society. But beyond this, pedagogy illuminates the dialogical and dynamic dimensions of the process of social transformation, aspects that must be foregrounded in any authentic democratic movement. In this regard, emancipatory pedagogy implicitly suggests a framework for social movement generally. The pedagogy in common that we have described in this context is the name both for the explicit principles of teaching that can help to build a new world and for the unsettling experience of learning that remakes all of us in the process.

CHAPTER 8

Steps Forward

Organization and Action

Although we have outlined some basic principles of governance, pedagogy, and curriculum that should frame a contemporary democratic approach to schooling, the exact shape that such schools should take cannot be specified outside of a collective struggle against neoliberalism and a collective imagination of alternatives. This is partly because it is impossible to see beyond existing enclosures except from the standpoint of a concrete struggle against them and partly because the building of new collective and democratic structures has to take place through a collective process; no one can completely describe such structures beforehand. Furthermore, against the overwhelmingly positivistic and technicist determination of schooling in the present—obsessed with specifying optimally efficient administrative and pedagogical processes—a new common school movement should remain partly in the fluid space of struggle and imagination and look to next steps rather than fully anticipating the final destination. An important question, then, is what this process of transition should look like, and what these next steps might be. In this chapter, we consider key principles and modes of engagement that we believe will be helpful in furthering the emerging organization and praxis of a new common school movement.

Guiding Principles

As we have described, it is crucial for this movement to confront neoliberalism directly as the central material and ideological frame for education in the present. In contrast to putatively progressive efforts that seek to make the best of the fragmentation of the public system by proposing "social justice–oriented" charters, and in contrast to liberal critics who limit their analyses to pointing out widening gaps in access and opportunity, we argue that a movement for democratic schooling must understand and denounce the logic of austerity and corporate control that lies behind contemporary education and school reform, as part of a broader reconstruction of society—that is, the shift from elite to common control over economic, political, and cultural institutions. Furthermore, in contrast to those who advocate a guerrilla tactics of subversion in the form of smuggling in elements of critical pedagogy and curriculum around the edges of the accountability regime, we believe that an organized movement is necessary—which seeks not just to evade or subvert the status quo in education but to challenge it directly and to construct alternatives that can replace it. Finally, in contrast to radicals who focus solely on the financial system or the war machine, we believe that the struggle over education, including and perhaps especially K–12 schooling, is central to any democratic transformation of society.

A movement, then, that seeks concretely to transform education will need to have an informed analysis of the historical and political conditions that have produced the current situation, a willingness to name and confront its adversary, and an interest in schooling as more than arbitrary site of struggle—that is, an understanding of education as uniquely generative of social meanings and possibilities. In addition, such a movement needs to have a clear position on the state and on the possibilities and limits of public schooling as a system. Against the impulse of some anarchists and autonomists to flee from the state entirely, we believe that the public-private distinction is significant and consequential and that an organized system of public schooling should be preserved, even as it is radically transformed. A simple refusal of state schooling, after all, can lead to micro-solutions that end up looking suspiciously like the entrepreneurial experiments of the anti-public charter boosters. At the same time, the radical reconstruction of the public, including public schooling, will need to be fundamental and to take place from the bottom up—against the regimes of austerity, accountability, containment, and stratification that currently define schooling. This implies that a new common school movement will need to think of ways to occupy and reorganize—on a collective and systemwide scale—the infrastructure of public schooling, and to do so on the basis of the distributed leadership of the community.

In addition, the terms within which such a movement thinks will need to be more than technical, economic, or even (narrowly) political. As it considers alternatives, a new common school movement will need to reimagine the epistemological, cultural, and curricular frameworks of education. As it challenges consolidated modes of authority with regard to governance and administration, this movement will also need to confront the dominant ways of knowing and being that currently set the limits of the meanings of teaching and learning. In this sense, it will be a philosophical movement as much as a political one, to the extent that it opens up for public and popular consideration the problem—urgent and yet persistently foreclosed in the present—of the *purpose* of education. Organizationally, this movement will need to invent forums for dialogue in which students, parents, teachers, and community members can interrupt entrenched forms of knowledge production and distribution and engage alternatives.

In addition to challenging the reification of knowledge produced by standardized testing, which breaks meaning into procedure, a new common school movement will need to challenge the *whiteness* of education—not just in terms of dispositions toward students but also in terms of the epistemological foundation of school knowledge. Globally, neoliberal austerity expresses and reproduces the problematic of coloniality; a truly democratic educational movement will need to upset the racism that decides what knowing and learning are and that centers white and Eurocentric forms of these. As the old "sorting machine" of school decomposes into a racist containment of black and brown students in preparation for semipermanent marginalization within the flux of an uncertain service economy and prison state, a radical educational movement will need to confront the violent ontology that determines these students as mere objects or disposable instances of "bare life." This means that this movement will need a process for investigating and confronting racism as a fundamental principle of actually existing education and neoliberalism itself. Breaking with the violence in the cultural order of the explicit curriculum and with the systematic injury expressed in the school-to-prison pipeline set in motion by hyperdiscipline, as well as with the accountability regime, this movement will need to participate in a broader emancipatory and decolonial project of liberation.

Strategies and Tactics

In the suggestions for organizing that follow, we partly build from efforts already under way, while also suggesting new initiatives. However, the ideas presented here aim not to generate action arbitrarily but to begin a process of educational transformation that heads in the direction that our larger argument in this book has sketched out: against neoliberal schooling and toward a new educational commons. This is not a comprehensive account; it is a set of starting points that can generate additional ideas for action.

1. Action from the Bottom Up

Educational advocacy and activism currently aim to mobilize specific communities to influence the crafting of legislation or the implementation of policy by elites. Advocates fight for rule changes governing funding, curriculum, accountability, and so on, or for their preferred candidates for state and federal appointments. While these efforts can modulate dominant regimes for the governance of schools and the shape of pedagogy, they cannot fundamentally alter them, since these campaigns accept current decision-making structures as unalterable. By contrast, we argue that a new common school movement should struggle as much for new participatory decision-making processes as for the specific content of policy or curriculum. In addition, such a movement should depend on the power of people involved in schools—students, parents, teachers, and community members—rather than on the goodwill of elites. Against the proven determination of the managers of the educational system not to deviate from the neoliberal consensus, not to mention the long history of schooling as an essential tool for the reproduction of class-racial domination, only a broad-based and militant popular movement is capable of realizing fundamental change and transformation.

In addition to focusing on building a popular base, a democratic challenge to the status quo depends on increased assertiveness from constituent groups. We believe that the time has come to move from the expression of discontent to action and that this shift should be coordinated among communities. In fact, there is evidence that such a shift is already beginning to take place. For instance, new groups of parents have formed to promote opposition to the accountability regime and to resist excessive testing of students.[1] Alliances of parents and teachers have formed in many locations to challenge the corporate schooling agenda—in particular, as it is expressed in the closure of neighborhood schools, the proliferation of charters, and gentrification. There is even an indication that educational researchers are becoming more willing to take a stand against the hegemonic consensus, through the formation of new working groups aimed at allying with the community and denouncing corporate-driven school reform.[2]

These efforts ought to be continued and coordinated. In addition, student organizing against neoliberalism in the university can be linked to work in the schooling context. In the wake of the Occupy movement, many important university-based projects, strikes, and protests have developed, which have challenged both the commodification of knowledge and the mortgaging of students' futures. Connecting this work to campaigns against the corporatization of K–12 schooling can reveal more fully the overall function of the corporatization of education within capitalism's new "knowledge economy" while also potentially building bridges between differently affected communities. Beyond this, the struggle over the schools ought to be more directly centered within global social justice and democracy movements. As global austerity has been ratcheted up in the wake of the debt crisis, promising new left movements have emerged. It is important for activists in these movements to recognize the crucial role played by schools in creating a laboratory for social futures and the central cultural-political role played in this context by youth. In addition, taking schooling seriously is an important step in taking seriously the concerns and conditions of existence of communities of color that are often marginalized even on the left.

2. Encuentros *for a Different Education*

For a popular movement to transform education to move forward, there has to be a forum in which basic dialogue can take place among participants. A new democratic schooling cannot be fashioned out of whole cloth but should be worked out by those most concerned with and affected by it. At the same time, collective dialogue already begins the pedagogical process in itself, since the sharing, discussion, and debate that must occur across communities on this question begin an alternative educational process and suggest models for formal approaches to pedagogy that might be instituted in schools. Recent popular uprisings globally, from Tahrir Square to Oakland, California, have been the occasion for the development of spontaneous communities in resistance, which have included as a crucial component a cooperative or auto-educational aspect, as movements have leveraged the expertise of participants to understand the political context and to propose alternatives. However, for our purposes, an even more useful precedent may be the model of the Zapatista *encuentro*: a popular, non-hierarchical gathering of diverse communities and organizations focused on advancing discussion around a particular issue. The intercontinental Zapatista *encuentros* against neoliberalism that took place in the 1990s brought together constituencies not previously in dialogue and sparked a wave of organizational energy that contributed importantly to the alter-globalization movement. Based on a "politics of listening and dignity,"[3] the *encuentro* disrupts the given distribution of authority on social and political questions, which privileges elites, by inviting the contributions of diverse communities in struggle while also aiming to forge an organized and coordinated plan of revolutionary action.

In the North American context, it is crucial for an organized alternative forum for discussion on education to be established outside of the official circuits of policy, media, and academic debate. A series of large-scale, community-based meetings, taking place at first outside of the schools themselves, could serve the initial purpose of indicating that a different kind of conversation around education is possible—beyond the grim pronouncements of neoliberal politicians or the anemic proposals of liberal academics. If such *encuentros* brought together parents, children, teachers, radical scholars, and activists, it could be the occasion for a set of reciprocal "teach-ins."[4] Analyses of the role and meaning of education could be shared from diverse perspectives, and suggestions for alternative forms of schooling could be proposed. This would be a chance for the pedagogies of the home, and the cultural wealth of communities of color, to be immediately shared and explored, rather than indirectly anticipated by teachers.[5] In addition, this would allow important critical-theoretical tools—such as analyses of neoliberalism and coloniality—to be shared with those who have been most affected by these processes.

In terms of curriculum, these forums might undertake the audacious task of considering what it is that students ought to be taught—free from the official common sense of state standards and the inherited presuppositions of decades of formal schooling. Although critical educators have spent a good deal of time investigating the "hidden curriculum," the idea that the *overt* curriculum—content knowledge itself—might be fundamentally rethought has not often been seriously entertained. Going beyond multiculturalism's effort to interrupt the monocultural narratives that have historically served as the foundation for textbooks and standards, the question of curriculum ought to be opened at a more basic level: recognizing the colonial determination of what counts as knowledge within the traditional disciplines, what do we think—*starting from scratch*—students ought to learn, and what do we think learning is? The popular *encuentros* suggested here could be occasions for those who have been excluded from this conversation to offer their suggestions and analyses and to begin the process of remaking education from the ground up. Diverse communities have crucial knowledge and ways of knowing that might be centered within a new common school movement, as well as crucial views on what it is important to learn. A truly radical dialogue in education needs to move through these basic epistemological questions, engaging regular people in producing what would be no less than a contemporary radical-popular philosophy of education.

3. Interrupting the Neoliberal Fantasy

Ideologically, the success of neoliberalism depends in large part on its foreclosure of alternatives—the sense it gives that there are no other options to its dominative order. This twisted "realism" is not new to capitalism, which always seeks to portray other visions of how to organize society as hopelessly utopian, but in the present, this is taken to a new level, as neoliberalism seeks to make good on this old promise: to subsume social life entirely and to make the market the sole model and measure for doing and being. In this context, capitalism captures subjects less through what it has them believe, and more through its enclosure of the possibilities for coherent relationships and action in the first place. Thus, in schools, the neoliberal accountability apparatus works less through securing participants' unfailing conviction that the measurements it incessantly produces accurately reflect real learning than through controlling all of the senses and procedures that determine what education *means* to begin with. Even though they may not necessarily believe that testing is always accurate or useful, teachers and students nevertheless find it very difficult to imagine a kind of learning that isn't always referred to or dependent on the test. In this way, accountability in education, and neoliberalism more generally, works as a kind of fantasy that *structures reality* for subjects, whether or not they "believe" in it.[6] As Theodor Adorno recognized, the allure of positivism (which drives standardized testing and curricular standardization) comes from the false promise of certainty and solidity in a world rendered abstract through the principle of economic exchange applied to everything. A new common school movement must displace the false promise of solidity and certainty of numbers with the actual promise of a better material world.

As the movement for a new common school moves from the stage of dialogue and discussion to the stage of action, it will need to find ways to intervene in schools themselves to interrupt this fantasy. Earlier, we discussed the necessity of bold challenges to the accountability regime and to the proliferation of standardized testing. But beyond refusals of the tests themselves, educators will need to confront the increasingly pervasive scripting of the curriculum and to consider ways to institute the kinds of projects conceptualized in the collective dialogues just described. One tactic that would be useful in this effort is what might be called a *curricular strike*. In a curricular strike, teachers would refuse altogether (for a set period) to follow the official curriculum and would instead implement projects and conversations not already given by the standards and answerable to the goals set by the educational *encuentros* and to the imagination of the educator. Although critical education has long argued for authentic engagement of students against the narrowness of the official curriculum, it has not reckoned with the current depth of control, and it has not generally contemplated the uses of collective defiance. But eventually open resistance will be necessary to break the spell of neoliberal accountability, if only to show quite simply that something different can happen in schools. If these strikes are successful in building courage and resistance, in a further step, educators and community members might undertake *school occupations*, understood not in the sense of the Occupy movement but rather in the sense of the Argentine worker occupations of abandoned factories: that is, as a process of appropriation in which those already at work at a site restart it and redirect it through a collective and democratic process—to restore the possibility of genuine productivity.

In the school occupation, teaching and learning would not be stopped but rather reimagined. At this stage, the point would be to begin to implement a more genuinely democratic education rather than merely to refuse the given. Obviously, such a step would be much more successful with the participation of the administration, and so an important element of the campaign we outline here is to work to enroll principals, other administrators, and classified staff in the movement. This opens a larger battle over governance, which might then extend to the regional level. In the first instance, however, local administrators responsible for ensuring the compliance and orderly functioning of individual schools will need to be awakened to a deeper sympathy and responsibility. While defections may seem unlikely at the outset, it is possible that as the movement strengthens, its momentum may help to convince administrators that their future lies with those with whom they share the space of the school and the possibility of community.

The structure of the current official school-community interface provides many opportunities for a struggle over the framing of teaching and learning, opportunities that are generally lost since the foundation for engagement is not yet in place. School advisory councils, parent-teacher associations, and campus support committees are all potential sites for radical organizing. However, useful interventions in these sites depend on the articulation of a broader political and philosophical framework, since questions about basic purposes and politics of education are otherwise impossible or ignored. Schools in which significant actions have taken place might become nodes in broader districtwide or regional coordination efforts. Nonschool community centers can become headquarters for campaigns and projects targeting the schools themselves. Furthermore, teacher-education programs, which have significant relationships with districts, are also important sites for struggle. The left-liberalism of many university schools of education ought to be pressed, in spite of itself, toward an insurgent engagement with communities. A good number of students and faculty are ready for just such a shift, and the backlash that would be generated by a concerted militancy against the accepted limits of teacher education would itself provide an excellent "teaching moment" regarding the structure of the system and the limits of the liberal imagination.

Conclusion

Starting from the interventions just described, a larger movement could then be built, within and beyond schools, as part of a broader reconstruction of society against neoliberalism. An important opening in education is the testing epidemic, which is already an important front for activism and can provide a wedge with which to mobilize and politicize movement participants.[7] However, what would distinguish

the organizing effort that we describe, and give it a special energy, is its focus on basic educational meanings and purposes. Gadflies like Alfie Kohn are correct in their criticisms of particular educational policies and practices, but their narrow focus on excesses and outrages leaves unanalyzed the underlying logic of capital and coloniality of which the accountability movement is only one expression, and this narrow focus does not open up basic political and pedagogical problems for the democratic imagination. Even critical theorists often lapse into an easy dialectic in which schools are characterized as, alternately, sites of domination and sites of emancipation. Although it is true that schools are a crucial site in which oppressed and marginalized groups have struggled for a limited degree of access and inclusion, at the same time schooling has been largely determined—historically and in the present—by the imperative of class-racial domination. The *public* in the public schools that we argue should be defended is not quite an existing reality of the common, but rather the site itself of struggle: the public should be defended as the privileged territory for the opening of a movement that would need to *invent* democracy, *against* a system of schooling that has for the most part parodied and persecuted it.

◆

CODA

Common Movements in Action

In this book, we have proposed a new vision and direction for emancipatory education globally. We have argued for recovering the progressive elements of the original common school movement and for defending and reimagining the value and organization of public education beyond neoliberalism. We have called for rethinking the purposes and social role of schooling to facilitate common labor and property for common benefit. We have suggested an alternative to the instrumental rationality and colonial legacies of thought by offering a vision of a pedagogy and curriculum in common. We have also provided an opening to reconceptualize educational leadership, finance, and teacher labor in terms of expanding the common. We want to emphasize that this project is about contributing to building a broad social movement of which education is one part. Recently educational activism has been a crucial terrain on which people have not only challenged neoliberalism but also put forward visions of critical education that emphasize socially engaged aspects of teaching and learning. Here, we highlight six key ongoing educational struggles against neoliberal education and for critical education to show how these struggles can be expanded and built on toward a new common school movement and a new commons. How can movements and projects not just challenge neoliberal education and not just build critical education but also build the commons?

From the Penguin Revolution
to the Chilean Winter

On September 11, 1973, General Augusto Pinochet overthrew the democratically elected government of Chile in a US-backed coup. Widely seen as the first experiment in radical neoliberal restructuring, the dictatorship implemented vast privatization schemes, which included replacing the public education system with a system of vouchers and privatizing the higher education sector. Even after the restoration of democracy, Chile's education system remains mired in this model. After decades of financial draining of public school resources and declining public schools, students in 2006 initiated the Penguin Revolution, named for their school uniforms. Students demanded an end to the system of municipal management that limited public control and allowed private and public corporations to dominate the education system. The neoliberal educational policy resulted in dire inequalities that benefited the rich and hurt everyone else. The 2006 protests included takeovers and occupations of schools and strikes by students that were, in turn, supported by strikes in multiple sectors. Many demands of the protesters were met by the government, but the Pinguinos also made challenging neoliberal education as a whole a central political issue and set the stage for the Chilean Winter protests of 2011. The Chilean Winter protesters continued to demand an end to municipal control, reform of the voucher system to restrict for-profit schools, implementation of public control and public support for secondary and higher education, reform of the admissions process, the creation of an intercultural university, and a moratorium on the creation of new voucher and charter schools. Although progress has been made in forcing the government to restrict for-profit education, the struggle for public education and against the radical neoliberal model continues. The world must learn a lesson from Chile's experience, and Chile's students are teaching it.

The Struggle for Social Justice
High School in Chicago

On May 13, 2001, fourteen parents and community members in the predominantly Mexican American community of Little Village launched a hunger strike to demand a new high school for their community. After nineteen days, the Chicago Public Schools agreed to build the school. The activists maintained their agenda for community control and led the design of the new school. The result was a campus with four small schools, including Social Justice High School. The school design focused on the relationship between learning and broader social, cultural, and political struggles for justice. The curriculum, inspired by the critical pedagogy of Paulo Freire, also emphasizes university preparation and one of the campuses focuses on science and mathematics. In 2009, the first students graduated from the school. Struggles continue over the teacher workforce and the extent to which the community, as opposed to the mayor, has control of the school. This struggle has taken place in the context of and despite the radical neoliberal restructuring of the Chicago Public Schools and this system's aggressive expansion of privatization and chartering, turnarounds, and corporate models of management. This indicates the power of direct action and the possibility that a small group of dedicated citizens working together can achieve important reform and the implementation of critical pedagogy.

Test Refusal in Seattle

Throughout the George W. Bush and Barack Obama administrations, standardized testing has been the basis for a system of financial and organizational rewards and punishments for schools. Schools, teachers, and students facing the greatest challenges have been punished for their test scores, while those with the greatest privileges have been rewarded for inheriting socially valued knowledge, tastes, and dispositions—that is, cultural capital. Standardized tests are being used not only to justify regressive funding but also to attack teacher job security and collective bargaining rights and to redefine teacher-preparation programs in ways that limit critical thinking, educational theory, and understandings of history and social context. In the context of punishing high-stakes testing, in which schools have had funds cut over scores or been subject to closure and untested reforms, teachers, students, and parents have gotten fed up. At the beginning of 2013, Seattle teachers refused to administer the district's MAP (Measures of Academic Progress) test, and there were indications that the Seattle protests might spread to other districts. Although refusing standardized testing is a hopeful step, it is important for teachers to highlight the cultural politics of the curriculum and the relationship between what is taught and learned and broader social, cultural, political, and economic forces and struggles. It is also crucial for the test refusal movement not to be co-opted by corporate school reformers and used as a basis for leaving poorly performing charters and other unproven privatization schemes unaccountable to the public.

The Chicago Teachers Union Strike

Chicago has endured a century of failed corporate school reforms. Among the most recent is one of the most aggressive privatization schemes to have reopened schools as charters. These "turnarounds" have closed schools and fired teachers. Chicago is a so-called urban portfolio district, meaning that the model for reform is "churn" or "creative destruction." Chicago has been taking the lead in setting the stage for a future two-tiered public system in which the schools of the working class and poor become money-making machines for investors. Within this system, money is saved by firing and burning out teachers to keep pay low. Meanwhile, the schools of the poorest students on the west and south sides of the city languish in terrible condition. The teachers' union is the main obstacle to this contracting scheme through its protection of experienced and certified teachers. In 2011, Mayor Rahm Emanuel and neoliberal groups succeeded in getting state legislation to restrict the strike capacity of the Chicago Teachers Union. A strike could only be launched with 75 percent of the teachers voting for it. Supporters of this legislation bragged that the CTU would never be able to strike again. The mayor broke the teachers' contract for annual raises and imposed a longer school day without compensation while promising to close and charter hundreds of schools. Emanuel and the other corporate school reformers waged a relentless teacher- and union-bashing campaign. Leaders of the Caucus of Rank and File Educators (CORE) organized the teachers to strike. Chicago teachers nearly unanimously supported the strike, and in September 2012, about 50,000 teachers filled the Chicago Loop. What was remarkable about the strike was not only that the teachers won a favorable contract against organized and well-funded hostility and propaganda from business groups and the mayor but also that the CORE leadership made use of the strike to highlight the broader political and economic stakes of Chicago's corporate school reform, including issues of poverty, privatization, and de-democratization. The strike inspired many other teachers' strikes and became a symbol of teachers' power and resistance in the face of a hostile national climate for unions, public workers, and the very idea of the public good.

The Citizen Schools of Porto Alegre

Since 1989, the city of Porto Alegre in Brazil has made critical pedagogy the basis for its education system. The system's critical approach to curriculum and pedagogy follows the work of Paulo Freire. This system of democratic organization extends even to a participatory budgeting process. These citizen schools make learning a matter of "reading the world," linking knowledge to the broader historical, social, political, and economic forces and struggles informing it. The process of problem-posing education has become the basis for community engagement and transformation. The citizen schools are a crucial model of critical pedagogy in action. Scholars and activists from around the world have visited the schools and written about their inspiring successes.

The Maple Spring Quebec Student Uprising

In the spring of 2012, students all over the Canadian province of Quebec participated in what has been called "the longest and largest student strike in the history of North America" and "the biggest act of civil disobedience in Canadian history." Upward of 300,000 students boycotted their classes, shutting down colleges and universities all over the province. Despite the efforts of authorities to use emergency ordinances to shut down the protests, a series of continuous mass public demonstrations were held consisting of hundreds of thousands of people from all walks of life, including secondary students, parents, union members, and citizens joining in solidarity. On May 25, 2012, alone, half a million people filled the streets of Montreal. The strike was ignited by a proposal to raise college and university tuition by 75 percent over five years or from $2,319 to $3,793 by 2017. However, the strike quickly transformed into a broader movement against the dismantling of the public and social contract in Quebec; against the corporate control, privatization, and de-funding of public education; and against the steady expansion of inequality and austerity across the province. The particular demand for affordable and publicly controlled higher education came to stand for a far more universal and fundamental defense of social democracy and with it possibilities for a common future rooted in justice and equality.

Each of the examples above highlights different social and political struggles over the educational commons across diverse geographical contexts. In Chile, students fought to reverse a vast and at the time unprecedented enclosure of the common good of the schools. They have challenged the voucher system, the disinvestment in public schools, and the turning of students into debt servants through dramatic displays of solidarity and educational occupations. In Chicago, the Little Village hunger strike and social movement represent a struggle over the distribution of resources and the organization of schooling and curriculum in the community. The movement was able to leverage its collective agency to establish an ongoing role in local school governance. In Seattle, teachers, students, and citizens have made explicit the need for commoning accountability and pedagogy beyond standardization and reductive testing. In Porto Alegre, the citizen schools have put into action the principles of a common pedagogy and common schooling as participatory democracy. In Montreal, students have demanded that funding for public higher education remains a common, as opposed to a private, matter and have exerted their collective aspirations through the occupation of urban space, providing a vivid example of the production of urban and educational commons.

To realize a broader vision for a new common school movement, national and local struggles like the ones described above need to be expanded and connected globally. These struggles need to learn from one another. The enclosures we have outlined throughout this text demand the creation of new networks and affiliations that link diverse struggles to the enactment of the global commons. For example, US teachers' unions can deepen their struggle against neoliberal education by learning from the critical pedagogical projects in Porto Alegre and street mobilizations and lessons of popular power articulated in Chile and Quebec. Most importantly, we need to find new ways of linking together these various struggles for common labor, common curriculum, common pedagogy, and common control over education. One of the ways power is reproduced globally today is through the privatization and fragmentation of our politics so that our shared condition and commonality are lost and subverted. A new common school movement must center education as a fundamental element in realizing a future beyond encroaching authoritarianism and against the planetary destruction guaranteed by predatory capitalism. This requires enacting the global commons.

The struggle against the enclosure of education and for knowledge in common must be linked to efforts to take ownership and control of knowledge-making institutions, to remake schools as a crucial stage and preparation for common labor for common benefit, and to end the labor-management divide inside schools. This is simultaneously a political, economic, cultural, pedagogical, and philosophical project. It requires a radical imagination and a willingness to challenge the elite consensus on schooling, the public, and democracy. And it requires the participation of diverse sectors, from students, teachers, and communities to intellectuals, researchers, and cultural workers. While neoliberalism and its representatives may appear to have the upper hand for the moment, the false consensus they incessantly proclaim belies a large and diverse groundswell of opposition globally, which is growing stronger every day. It is our hope that the analysis and proposals we have offered in this book can in some measure fortify the global movement for a common schooling as it confronts the difficult challenges that will emerge in the course of struggle.

Notes

Preface

1. Michael Hardt and Antonio Negri, *Commonwealth* (Cambridge: Harvard University Press, 2009).

Chapter 1

1. The hijacking of the language of social justice by neoliberal education can be found repeatedly in the speeches of US Secretary of Education Arne Duncan. Kenneth Saltman heard Duncan equate privatization initiatives with efforts for social justice at the Commercial Club of Chicago Renaissance Schools Fund's "Free to Choose, Free to Succeed: The New Market in Public Education" event in Chicago on May 6, 2008. See, for example, "Secretary of Education Arne Duncan's 'Call to Service Lecture at Harvard University,'" available at the US Department of Education website at http://www.ed.gov/news/speeches/call-service-lecture-harvard -university. For criticism of this misuse of the language of social justice in education see, for example, Henry Giroux, *Education and the Crisis of Public Values* (New York: Peter Lang, 2011).

2. Despite the long critical educational tradition in the United States, ranging from the reconstructionists to critical pedagogy, most progressive magazines such as *The Nation* and *Harper's* tend to largely exclude the critical education perspective, instead promoting liberal views.

3. Tooley has also authored a book framing feminism as a threat to women globally. James Tooley, *The Mis-Education of Women* (Chicago: Ivan R. Dee Publisher, 2003). Tooley's position that women's place is in the home and that feminism threatens masculine domination of the economy should be taken seriously

in relation to his call for a corporate fast food model of education in poor countries. He demonstrates a consistent commitment to inequality that spans economic class and gender. That the World Bank has so aggressively embraced Tooley's "scholarship" should not come as a great surprise to those familiar with the World Bank's history of imposing debt servitude, privatization, and other aspects of "structural adjustment" on poor nations while helping to enrich private interests in rich nations.

4. See Zygmunt Bauman, *The Individualized Society* (Malden, MA: Blackwell, 2001).

5. Linda Darling-Hammond, *The Flat World and Education* (New York: Teachers College Press, 2010), 28.

6. Darling-Hammond, 26.

7. Stanley Aronowitz, *Against Schooling and for an Education That Matters* (Boulder, CO: Paradigm Publishers, 2008).

8. On the need for an intertwined theory of economic distribution and cultural recognition, see Nancy Fraser, *Justice Interruptus* (New York: Routledge 1997), particularly Chapters 1 and 3, and the more recent *Scales of Justice* (New York: Columbia, 2009), in which she expands the economic and cultural matrix to include political representation.

Chapter 2

1. Garrett Hardin, "The Tragedy of the Commons," *Science* 162 (1968): 1243–1248.

2. David Harvey, "The Future of the Commons," *Radical History Review* (Winter 2011): 101–107.

3. Elinor Ostrum, *Governing the Commons: The Evolution of Institutions for Collective Action* (Cambridge, MA: Cambridge University Press, 1990).

4. Karl Marx, *Capital*, Vol. 1 (New York: Penguin Books, 1976), 873–931.

5. Peter Linebaugh, *The Magna Carta Manifesto* (Berkeley, CA: University of California Press, 2008).

6. Silvia Federici, *Caliban and the Witch: Women, the Body, and Primitive Accumulation* (New York: Autonomedia, 2004).

7. Slavoj Žižek, *First as Tragedy, Then as Farce* (New York: Verso, 2009), 91.

8. See Carlo Vercellone, "Cognitive Capitalism and Models for the Regulation of Wage Relations: Lessons from the Anti-CPE Movement," in *Toward a Global Autonomous University*, edited by Edu-factory Collective (New York: Autonomedia, 2009), 119–124.

9. For essential postcolonial and decolonial analyses of globality, which are crucial to start from in framing a viable contemporary
understanding of the common, see Enrique Dussel, *Beyond Philosophy: Ethics, History, Marxism, and Liberation Theology* (Lanham,
MD: Rowman & Littlefield, 2003); Walter D. Mignolo, *The Darker Side
of Western Modernity: Global Futures, Decolonial Options* (Durham,
NC: Duke University Press, 2011); and Chandra Talpade Mohanty,
Feminism without Borders: Decolonizing Theory, Practicing Solidarity
(Durham, NC: Duke University Press, 2003).

10. See Saskia Sassen, *Globalization and Its Discontents: Essays
on the New Mobility of People and Money* (New York: The New Press,
1998).

11. Joel Kovel, *The Enemy of Nature: The End of Capitalism or
the End of the World?* (New York: Zed Books, 2002).

12. See above all Thomas L. Friedman, *The World Is Flat: A Brief
History of the Twenty-First Century* (New York: Farrar, Straus &
Giroux, 2005).

Chapter 3

1. Howard Zinn, *A People's History of the United States* (New
York: The New Press, 2003), 162.

2. Zinn notes, "In Philadelphia, working-class families lived
fifty five to a tenement, usually one room per family, with no garbage removal, no toilets, no fresh air or water.... In New York you
could see the poor lying in the streets with the garbage. There were
no sewers in the slums, and filthy water drained into yards and
alleys, into the cellars where the poorest of the poor lived, bringing
with it a typhoid epidemic in 1837, typhus in 1842. In the cholera
epidemic of 1832, the rich fled the city; the poor stayed and died"
(162).

3. Zinn, 164.

4. We draw here from Wayne J. Urban and Jennings L. Wagoner
Jr., *American Education: A History* (New York: Taylor & Francis,
2009); and Samuel Bowles and Herbert Gintis, *Schooling in Capitalist America* (New York: Basic Books, 2011).

5. Horace Mann, *The Republic and the School* (New York: Teachers College Press, 1957), 86.

6. Ibid., 64.

7. Ibid., 87.

8. See John Bellamy Foster, "Education and the Structural
Crisis of Capitalism," *Monthly Review* 63, no. 3 (2011). Available at http://monthlyreview.org/2011/07/01/education-and
-the-structural-crisis-of-capital.

9. Raymond Callahan, *Education and the Cult of Efficiency* (Chicago: University of Chicago Press, 1962), 152.

10. Ibid., 58.

11. See Bellamy Foster, "Education and the Structural Crisis of Capitalism."

12. Callahan, 121.

13. John Dewey, *Democracy and Education* (New York: The Free Press, 1916), 87.

14. Bellamy Foster, "Education and the Structural Crisis of Capitalism."

15. Ibid.

16. For this history, see Howard Zinn, *A People's History of the United States.*

17. Bowles and Gintis, *Schooling in Capitalist America.*

18. Linda Darling-Hammond, *The Flat World and Education* (New York: Teachers College Press, 2010), 18.

19. Bellamy Foster, "Education and the Structural Crisis of Capitalism."

Chapter 4

1. Rajesh Makwana, "Global Inequality," report prepared for Share the World's Resources (2006). Available at http://www.stwr.org/poverty-inequality/global-inequality.html.

2. David McNally, "Slump, Austerity, and Resistance," *Socialist Register* 48 (2012).

3. These statistics concerning those that qualify as low-income and impoverished emerged out of analysis of the 2010 federal census and were widely reported in the media.

4. PEW Research Center, "One in 31 U.S. Adults Are Behind Bars, on Parole or Probation" (2009). Available at http://www.pewcenteronthestates.org/news_room_detail.aspx?id=49398.

5. Chris Hellman and Mattea Kramer, "Our Insanely Big $1 Trillion National Security Budget," *Mother Jones* (2012). Available at http://www.motherjones.com/politics/2012/05/national-securitybudget-1-trillion congress.

6. Bureau of Justice Statistics, *Prison Inmates at Midyear 2009: Statistical Tables.* Available at http://bjs.ojp.usdoj.gov/content/pub/pdf/pim09st.pdf.

7. Ruth Wilson Gilmore, *Golden Gulag: Prisons, Surplus, Crisis, and Opposition in Globalizing California* (Berkeley, CA: University of California Press, 2007).

8. See Joy James, *Resisting State Violence: Radicalism, Gender, and Race in U.S. Culture* (Minneapolis, MN: University of

Minnesota Press, 1996); and Angela Davis, *Abolition Democracy: Beyond Empire, Prisons, and Torture* (New York: Seven Stories, 2005).

9. Maurizio Lazzarato, *The Making of the Indebted Man*, translated by Joshua David Jordan (Cambridge, MA: Semiotext(e)/The MIT Press, 2012). On page 110, Lazzarato makes these similar points.

10. Silvia Federici, "Feminism and the Politics of the Commons" (2011). Available at http://www.commoner.org.uk/?p=113.

11. Our conception of a dual crisis of neoliberalism and neoliberal schooling draws on the ideas put forth by the Edu-factory Collective concerning the "double crisis" of the university and post-Fordism. See Edu-factory Collective, "The Double Crisis: Living on the Borders," *Edu-factory Journal*, Zero Issue (2010): 4–9.

12. Jeff Bryant, "Starving America's Schools," *National Education Association*. Available at http://www.ourfuture.org/files /documents/starving-schools-report.pdf.

13. Kenneth J. Saltman, *Capitalizing on Disaster: Taking and Breaking Public Schools* (Boulder, CO: Paradigm Publishers, 2007), Chapter 1.

14. Mark Fisher, *Capitalist Realism: Is There No Alternative?* (Washington, DC: Zero Books, 2009).

15. Harper's Index, *Harper's Magazine* (April 2012).

16. Lee Fang, "How Online Learning Companies Bought America's Schools," *The Nation* (December 2011). Available at http://www.thenation.com/article/164651/how-online-learning -companies-bought-americas-schools.

17. Stephanie Simon, "Privatizing Public Schools: Big Firms Eyeing Profits from U.S. K–12 Market," *Huffington Post* (August 2012). Available at http://www.huffingtonpost.com/2012/08/02 /private-firms-eyeing-prof_n_1732856.html.

18. Quoted in Fang.

19. UNICEF, "Measuring Child Poverty" (2012). Available at http://www.unicef-irc.org/publications/pdf/rc10_eng.pdf.

20. Kenneth C. Land, "2010 Child Well-Being Index" (2010). Available at http://fcd-us.org/resources/2010-child-well-being -index-cwi?doc_id=4642; Annie E. Casey Foundation (AEC). *America's Children, America's Challenge* (2011). Available at http://datacenter.kidscount.org/databook/2011/OnlineBooks /2011KCDB_FINAL.

21. For a variety of research reports that show the numerous shortcomings of the corporate reform movement, see the studies conducted by CREDO at Stanford University (http://credo.stanford .edu), the National Center for Education Policy at the University of Colorado (http://nepc.colorado.edu), and the Economic Policy Institute (www.epi.org). For broad overviews of the problems

associated with corporate reforms, see from a liberal perspective Linda Darling-Hammond, *The Flat World and Education* (New York: Teachers College Press, 2010), and from a critical perspective Kenneth J. Saltman, *The Failure of Corporate School Reform* (Boulder, CO: Paradigm Publishers, 2012).

22. Massimo De Angelis, "Obama Meets Lenin" (2009). Available at http://www.thecommoner.org.uk/?p=80.

23. Bureau of Labor Statistics (BLS), "Occupations with the Largest Growth," *Monthly Labor Review* (2012). Available at http://www.bls.gov/emp/ep_table_104.htm.

Chapter 5

1. David Harvey, "The Future of the Commons," *Radical History Review* (Winter 2011): 101–107.

2. Ibid.

3. See Linda Darling-Hammond, *The Flat World and Education* (New York: Teachers College Press, 2010) for abundant empirical evidence as to the destructive effects of these anti-teacher policies on the "quality" of teaching as measured by test outputs.

4. In saying "critically engaged," we are referring not to critical thinking as a problem-solving skill but rather to "critical" in the tradition of critical pedagogy, which takes up questions of knowledge in relation to broader power struggles, interests, and social structures.

5. Michael Hardt and Antonio Negri, *Commonwealth* (Cambridge, MA: Harvard University Press, 2009).

6. Michael Hardt, Antonio Negri, and David Harvey, "Commonwealth: An Exchange," *Artforum* 48 (November 2009): 210–221.

7. Harvey, 107.

8. Ibid.

9. Jacques Rancière, *Disagreement: Politics and Philosophy* (Minneapolis, MN: University of Minnesota Press, 1999).

10. Gloria Ladson Billings, "From Achievment Gap to Educational Debt," *Educational Researcher* 35, no. 7 (October 2006): 3–12.

11. See Kenneth J. Saltman, *The Failure of Corporate School Reform* (Boulder, CO: Paradigm Publishers, 2012).

12. Jeff Madrick, "The Entitlement Crisis That Isn't," *Harper's Magazine* (November 2012).

13. An FST has broad support even among hard-core neoliberals like Lawrence Summers; only the most regressive factions of the conservative and libertarian right oppose such a measure.

14. Richard Wolfe, *Democracy at Work: A Cure for Capitalism* (Chicago: Haymarket Books, 2012).

Chapter 6

1. Edward W. Said, *Culture and Imperialism* (New York: Vintage Books, 1993), 67.

2. See Walter D. Mignolo, *The Darker Side of Western Modernity* (Durham, NC: Duke University Press, 2011); and Aníbal Quijano, "Coloniality of Power, Eurocentrism, and Latin America," in *Coloniality at Large: Latin America and the Postcolonial Debate*, edited by Mabel Moraña, Enrique Dussel, and Carlos A. Jáuregui (Durham, NC: Duke University Press, 2008), 181–224.

3. Paolo Virno, *A Grammar of the Multitude*, translated by Isabella Bertoletti, James Cascaito, and Andrea Casson (Los Angeles: Semiotext(e), 2004).

4. Julian Vasquez Heilig, Keffrelyn D. Brown, and Anthony L. Brown, "The Illusion of Inclusion: A Critical Race Theory Textual Analysis of Race and Standards," *Harvard Educational Review* 82, no. 3 (2012): 403–424.

5. For this evocative notion, see Michael Hardt, "Prison Time," *Yale French Studies* 91 (1997): 64–79.

6. On punishment, see U.S. Department of Education, "New Data from U.S. Department of Education Highlights Inequities Around Teacher Experience, Discipline and High School Rigor." Available (consulted February 6, 2013) at http://www.ed.gov /news/press-releases. On push-outs, see Linda M. McNeil, "Faking Equity: High-Stakes Testing and the Education of Latino Youth," in *Leaving Children Behind: How "Texas-Style" Accountability Fails Latino Youth*, edited by Angela Valenzuela (Albany, NY: State University of New York Press, 2005), 57–111.

7. Noah De Lissovoy, "Decolonial Pedagogy and the Ethics of the Global," *Discourse: Studies in the Cultural Politics of Education* 31, no. 3 (2010): 279–293.

8. Paulo Freire, *Pedagogy of the Oppressed*, translated by Myra Bergman Ramos (New York: Continuum, 1996).

9. Studies demonstrating these processes include Stephen J. Ball, "The Teacher's Soul and the Terrors of Performativity," *Journal of Education Policy* 18, no. 2 (2003): 215–228; and Michael Peters, "Education, Enterprise Culture and the Entrepreneurial Self: A Foucauldian Perspective," *Journal of Educational Enquiry* 2, no. 2 (2001): 58–71.

10. Antonio Negri, "The Constitution of Time," part 1 in *Time for Revolution*, translated by Matteo Mandarini (New York: Continuum, 2003).

11. Noah De Lissovoy, "Education and Violation: Conceptualizing Power, Domination, and Agency in the Hidden Curriculum," *Race, Ethnicity and Education* 15, no. 4 (2012): 463–484.

12. Henry Giroux's emphasis on the pedagogical production of subjectivity and the need to produce democratic forms of identifications is long-standing. See, for example, *Border Crossings* (New York: Routledge, 2005), *Disturbing Pleasures* (New York: Routledge, 1994), and *Schooling and the Struggle for Public Life* (Minneapolis, MN: University of Minnesota Press, 1988), among other works.

13. Michael Hardt and Antonio Negri, *Commonwealth* (Cambridge, MA: Harvard University Press, 2009), 169.

14. See Edu-factory Collective, *Toward a Global Autonomous University: Cognitive Labor, the Production of Knowledge, and Exodus from the Education Factory* (New York: Autonomedia, 2009).

15. See Luis Urrieta Jr. and Margarita Machado-Casas, "Book Banning, Censorship, and Ethnic Studies in Urban Schools: An Introduction to the Special Issue," *Urban Review* 45, no. 1 (2013): 1–6.

16. Working in the tradition of Vygotsky, Barbara Rogoff has powerfully developed this idea. See her *Apprenticeship in Thinking: Cognitive Development in Social Context* (Oxford: Oxford University Press, 1990). See also L. S. Vygotsky, *Mind in Society: The Development of Higher Psychological Processes* (Cambridge, MA: Harvard University Press, 1978).

17. Jacques Rancière, *On the Shores of Politics*, translated by Liz Heron (London: Verso, 2007).

Chapter 7

Grateful acknowledgment is made for permission to revise and reprint portions of the following essay in this chapter: Noah De Lissovoy, "Pedagogy in Common: Democratic Education in the Global Era," *Educational Philosophy and Theory* 43, no. 10 (2011): 1119–1134.

1. Noel Gough, "Locating Curriculum Studies in the Global Village," *Journal of Curriculum Studies* 32, no. 2 (2000): 334.

2. See James A. Banks, "Diversity, Group Identity, and Citizenship Education in a Global Age," *Educational Researcher* 37, no. 3 (2008): 129–139; and Gloria Ladson-Billings, "New Directions in Multicultural Education: Complexities, Boundaries, and Critical Race Theory," in *Handbook of Research on Multicultural Education*, edited by James A. Banks and Cherry A. McGee Banks (San Francisco, CA: Jossey-Bass, 2004), 50–65.

3. John Dewey, *Democracy and Education* (New York: The Free Press, 1997 [1944]).

4. Useful accounts of these processes, however, are given respectively by Arjun Appadurai in *Fear of Small Numbers: An Essay*

on the Geography of Anger (Durham, NC: Duke University Press, 2006), and by Zygmunt Bauman in *Liquid Modernity* (Cambridge, UK: Polity, 2000).

5. John Dewey, *Experience and Education* (New York: Simon & Schuster, 1997 [1938]).

6. See, for instance, Ernest Morrell and Jeffrey M. R. Duncan-Andrade, "Promoting Academic Literacy with Urban Youth through Engaging Hip-Hop Culture," *The English Journal* 91, no. 6 (2002): 88–92.

7. Grace Lee Boggs, "Food for All: How to Grow Democracy," *The Nation* (September 21, 2009): 14–15.

8. Luis Armando Gandin and Michael W. Apple, "New Schools, New Knowledge, New Teachers: Creating the Citizen School in Porto Alegre, Brazil," *Teacher Education Quarterly* 31, no. 1 (2004): 173–198.

9. Massimo De Angelis, *The Beginning of History: Value Struggles and Global Capitalism* (London: Pluto Press, 2007), 23–24.

10. Dewey, *Democracy and Education*, 87.

Chapter 8

1. See, for instance, United Opt Out National (www.unitedoptout.com).

2. See, for instance, the Edu4 network (www.education4.org).

3. Mariana Mora, "The Imagination to Listen: Reflections on a Decade of Zapatista Struggle," *Social Justice* 30, no. 3 (2003): 17–31.

4. For an excellent description of the use of the encuentro organizing model in the US educational context, see Emmet Campos, "Crucibles of Cultural and Political Change: Postmodern Figured Worlds of Tejana/o Chicana/o Activism." PhD diss., University of Texas at Austin, 2011.

5. Dolores Delgado Bernal, "Learning and Living Pedagogies of the Home: The Mestiza Consciousness of Chicana Students," in *Chicana/Latina Education in Everyday Life: Feminista Perspectives on Pedagogy and Epistemology*, edited by Dolores Delgado Bernal, C. Alejandra Elenes, Francisca E. Godinez, and Sofia Villenas (Albany, NY: State University of New York Press, 2006), 113–132; Tara Yosso, "Whose Culture Has Capital? A Critical Race Theory Discussion of Community Cultural Wealth," *Race Ethnicity and Education* 8, no. 1 (2005): 69–91.

6. Žižek is the preeminent analyst of this notion of ideology as fantasy; see Slavoj Žižek, *The Sublime Object of Ideology* (London: Verso, 2008). For an excellent analysis of Žižek's argument, and an

application of it to the field of neoliberalism itself, see Jodi Dean, *Democracy and Other Neoliberal Fantasies: Communicative Capitalism and Left Politics* (Durham, NC: Duke University Press, 2009).

7. This can dramatically be seen in recent teacher boycotts of standardized tests—for instance, the boycott of a district-mandated test by high school teachers in Seattle.

Index

climate change, 15, 19
Clinton, Bill, 3–4
cognitive capitalism, 15–16
collectivity, 20; and decision
    making, 85; education and,
    86; Harvey on, 49–50
coloniality: challenging,
    92–93; *encuentros* and, 96
command, capitalism and, 75
the common, vi–vii; and
    collective property rights,
    49–50; communicative,
    17–18; ecological, 19; Mann
    and, 24; nature of, 12–13;
    postcolonial, 18–19; term,
    80; transnational, 16–17
common core curriculum, 8
common movements, 101–107
commons, 12–21; Hardt and
    Negri on, 52–53; nature of,
    13; need for, 9–11; renewed
    interest in, 38; social
    reproduction of, education
    and, 86–89; tragedy of, 13
common school movement:
    original, vii, 23–24.
    See also new common
    school movement
communication, 69, 79
communicative
    common, 17–18
community of equals, 79
community of learners, 78
consensus, 55
conservativism: and common
    school movement, 24;
    and public schooling, 1.
    See also neoliberalism
constructionism, 83
control: new common school
    movement and, 56–57;
    pedagogies of, 61
conversation, and
    pedagogy, 78–79
conviction, 55–56

corporate culture: history of,
    25, 28; and management,
    43–44; and profiteering,
    44–45; resistance to, 10
corporate model, 2–3,
    40–41; effects of, 51–52;
    liberalism and, 8–9;
    neoliberalism and, 30
Council for the Accreditation
    of Educator Preparation, 66
Counts, George, 27
creative destruction, 37, 104
creativity, 17, 51
critical consciousness, 9
critical pedagogy, 73, 78
critical theory: on education
    for social justice, 9–11;
    on inequality, 8
Cubberly, Elwood, 25
culture, commons
    of, 14, 62–64
culture wars, 71
curriculum, 80–89; corporate
    model and, 43; crisis of,
    69–73; *encuentros* and, 96;
    neoliberalism and, 71–72;
    reaction and, 71; rupture
    and, 75; strike against, 98

Darling-Hammond, Linda, 7
De Angelis, Massimo,
    14, 47, 87
decolonial theorists, 70
De Lissovoy, Noah, 75
democracy: Dewey and, 27;
    education and, 87–88; and
    governance, 60; term, 20,
    88
democratic potential, 10, 12
devaluation, strategic, 41–42
developing nations,
    privatization in, 3
development: in curriculum,
    82; uneven, 33
Dewey, John, 26–27, 76, 83

higher education,
alternatives to, 77
hip-hop, classroom
investigation of, 84
Hirsch, E. D., 8

imagination, 88; and
democracy, 20; enclosure
and, 15–16; versus
neoliberal fantasy,
97–99; and pedagogy, 77;
recommendations for, 63–64
immigration, 79
individualized society, 6
industrialized nations,
privatization in, 2–3
inequality, 33–34, 45
infrastructure, neoliberalism
and, 14, 36–37
internal nature,
commons of, 15
investigation, in
curriculum, 84–85
investment: in education
privatization and reform,
44–45; foreign direct, 3

Johnson, Lyndon B., 29

Katrina, Hurricane, 15, 42–43
Keynes, John
Maynard, 28, 32
King, Martin Luther, Jr., 29
Klein, Naomi, 42
knowledge: authority
and, 73; enclosure and,
15–16; *encuentros* and,
96; liberalism on, 6;
neoliberalism and, 69, 79
Kohn, Alfie, 100
Kozol, Jonathan, 58

labor, 18; collective, 49–50,
54; future occupations,
47–48; new common

school movement and,
59–64; of teachers, 50
labor unions. *See*
teachers' unions
Ladson-Billings, Gloria, 57–58
language, neoliberalism
and, 4, 108n1
Lazzarato, Maurizio, 36
leadership, distributed, 82, 92
liberalism, on education
for social justice, 6–9
Linebaugh, Peter, 14
livelihoods, new common
school movement and,
62–64
Lytle, Rob, 44

Mann, Horace, vii, 23–24
Maple Spring, 105–106
marginalized populations:
common school movement
and, 24; early public
education and, 27; in
postwar era, 28–29;
prison-industrial
complex and, 35, 62
market ideology, 2, 30–33,
40–41; authoritarianism
and, 35; in curriculum,
82; effects of, 68; and
management, 43–44;
TINA thesis and, 4, 32
Marx, Karl, 13–14, 17, 37
Marxian analytical
tradition, 12, 20
McNally, David, 33–34
measurement, effects
of, 67, 69, 72
military-industrial
complex, 28, 35;
recommendations for, 63
money, Harvey on, 50
morality, Mann and, 24
Morgan, J. P., 25
Moynihan, Daniel Patrick, 29

◆

About the Authors

Noah De Lissovoy is Assistant Professor of Cultural Studies in Education at the University of Texas at Austin. He is the author of *Power, Crisis, and Education for Liberation: Rethinking Critical Pedagogy*, which won the Critics' Choice Award from the American Educational Studies Association.

Alexander J. Means is Assistant Professor in the Department of Social and Psychological Foundations of Education at the State University of New York at Buffalo State College. He is the author of *Schooling in the Age of Austerity: Urban Education and the Struggle for Democratic Life*.

Kenneth J. Saltman is Professor of Educational Policy Studies and Research at DePaul University, where he teaches in the Social and Cultural Foundations of Education graduate program. He is the author most recently of *The Failure of Corporate School Reform*. He is a fellow of the National Education Policy Center.